T0381502

Cradled in the Arms of Love

Written and compiled by Naomi Kapplehoff

Order this book online at www.trafford.com
or email orders@trafford.com

Most Trafford titles are also available at major online book retailers.

Print information available on the last page.

ISBN: 978-1-4120-7671-5 (sc)

Trafford rev. 04/23/2015

North America & international
toll-free: 1 888 232 4444 (USA & Canada)
fax: 812 355 4082

DEDICATED TO

Our parents, Peter and Maria (Derksen) Wiens
Who gave us life, music and a Christian heritage;
And to Abram W. Martens
Who made her so happy in her retirement years.

I will meet you in the morning,
Just inside the Eastern Gate;
Then be ready, faithful pilgrim,
Lest with you it be too late.

If you hasten off to glory,
Linger near the Eastern Gate,
For I'm coming in the morning,
So you'll not have long to wait.

Keep your lamps all trimmed and burning,
For the Bridegroom watch and wait;
He'll be with us at the meeting,
Just inside the Eastern Gate.

O, the joy of that glad meeting,
With the saints who for us wait!
What a blessed, happy meeting,
Just inside the Eastern Gate.

Chorus:
I will meet you in the morning
I will meet you in the morning
Just inside the Eastern Gate over there;
I will meet you in the morning
I will meet you in the morning
I will meet you in the morning over there.

ACKNOWLEDGEMENTS

A project of this magnitude is never a one-person job. It has taken many people to bring this story to this point. At this time I would like to acknowledge the people who assisted me in one way or another. Many special thanks go out to my cousin, Mary Pauls, who immigrated to Canada with her parents and lived through the horrors of the Great Depression. Even now in her 80's, she could still remember back to that time period with great clarity. Thank you, Mary, for sharing your memories with me, so many times over the past few months.

The revisions of this book would have been more tedious if it was not for the help of my sisters Anna, Beth and Vi who offered to read what I had written and make suggestions. Your help was greatly appreciated. Thank you, Ken & Anna for all your input on information that pertains to the farming in general as well as sharing the farm house plans that you drew for another purpose.

Special thanks go to my brother, Ed and to Walter Isaak, who were willing to share with me their memories of what happened on September 25, 1961. Thanks you for casting light on the day that changed the dynamics of our family.

To all my many nieces and nephews who shared their memories of their grandmother – thank you!! You were an important part of her life.

Many special thanks go to Dianne Petrie and her mother, Norma Bruget, who read the manuscript for fluency and clarity.

There is one person, Madonna, who almost became a journalist during the McCarthy era. Thank you, Madonna, for helping me to keep a proper prospective on the various issues as they came up.

To Jack Peterson and Kathy Binkley, my carpool buddies, you helped me to see various issues from many different sides. I found these conversations to be very stimulating. Bobbie Bailey, you were greatly instrumental in the forming of this manuscript as you prayed with me during its formation that it would be a God-honoring story of my Mother. Thank you Bobbie!

I really need to thank my husband, Phil, for putting up with all the research that went on during the past six months. Your support and encouragement was greatly appreciated. You did a great job on the artwork that became the cover of this book long before this book even became a seed of a thought.

Last but not least, this project would not be complete without the permission of my brothers and sisters who wrote letters of tribute to our parents so many years ago. To the brothers and sisters who provided all those pictures with some of them being last minute pictures – thank you!

I cannot go on until I acknowledge my Aunts Njessa, Susie and Hulda who each had information to share about the days gone by both in Canada and Russia. Our lives are never complete without people like you.

To Marjorie Gorman Wiens, who recorded an interview with our Mother on her 75th birthday – thank you for being so insightful in doing this interview. Who knew that one day that information would be invaluable.

A very big thank you goes to my sister-in-law, Liz Sanderson and my brother, Vic, for being my cheering squad, encouraging me along the way. You're appreciation of family history has not gone unnoticed. My hat goes off to you. You have made this project entirely possible. An extra special thanks to you for putting up with the work and rewrites when it just never seemed to end.

Two other people have become such a great asset in the final finish of this project. To Patrick Callahan who served as a technical director, proofreader and prepress formatter for this project not once but twice – a double thanks. Without you it just wouldn't be done. A special thanks also goes to Patrick for designing the family website.

Just when I thought it was finished, Wendy Jensen entered the picture and took what I did shaping it into what it has become – a much more concise picture of our family. Wendy, your accomplishments in weeding down the words is so very much appreciated. Thank you so very much for the many hours spent in the library working on the editing of this book when you could have been out in the Wisconsin sun. Your work is a crowning and appreciated accomplishment in recording our family history for future generations.

The Family Trees of Peter Peter Wiens & Maria Georginia Derksen

Gerhard G. Derksen & Anna Andreas Pankratz Family

George	Justina	Anna
John	Sara	Elizabeth
Margaret	Agnes	Tina
Ella	**Maria** Henry	
	Susanna	

Peter Peter Wiens & Maria Eck Weddel

Sara Wiens	Justina Wiens	Margareta Wiens
	Lena Wiens	**Peter Wiens**

Maria Eck Weddel Wiens & Peter H. Pauls

Hans Pauls	Katharina Pauls	Mariechen Pauls
	Njessa Pauls	

The Family of Peter Peter Wiens & Maria Georgina Derksen

Lily	Herbert	Rose	Anna
Reuben	Edward	Violet	Elizabeth (Beth)
John	Victor	George	Naomi
	Melita		Blondina

The grandchildren and great grandchildren of Peter & Maria Wiens

1. Lily Florence Wiens & Lawrence Irvin Willems
   a. Iris Valerie Willems
   b. Heather Angela Willems & Dean Wiggins
      i. Kain Michel Wiggins   ii. Sadie Lyn Wiggins
      iii. Caydon Rence Wiggins iv. Kellen Aston Wiggins
2. Herbert Peter Wiens & Viola Patricia Willms
   a. Howard Keith Wiens & Cheri Lynn Weinhauer
      i. Julie Corine Wiens   ii. Camden Keith Wiens
               iii. Brenna Arlene Wiens
   b. Geraldine (Gerry) Jennifer Wiens
      i. Brandon James Wiens   ii. Katerina May Wiens
3. Rose Hildegard Wiens & Ernst Penner
   a. Tamara Cheryl Penner & Paul David Goodwin
      i. Matthew Joseph Goodwin   ii. Spencer William Goodwin
               iii. Kathrina Mae Goodwin
   b. Dana Andrew Penner & Robyn Louise Bowell
      i. Luke Peter Connor Penner   ii. Savannah Grace Penner
      ii. Micah Rose Sharon Penner   iv. Lauryn Faith Penner

4. Anna Grace Wiens & Kenneth Peter Kroeker

- a. Janet Kimberly Kroeker & Lorn Jeremy Gieck
  - i. Judith Charis Gieck   ii. Theodore Spencer Gieck
- b. Barbara Ann Kroeker & Kimberly Wayne Worthington
  - i. Alexander Jamin Worthington
- c. Robert Peter Kroeker & Patrica Marie Reynolds
  - i. Richelle Betty May Sauerberg
5. Reuben Peter Wiens & Sharon Dale Sibley
   - a. Travis Kent Wiens
   - b. Darren Kirk Wiens
6. Edward Peter Wiens & Donna Lynne Beaton
   - a. Emily Alison Wiens
7. Violet Viola Wiens & John Howard Parris
   - a. Justin Francis Parris & Rachel Deanna Filby
   - b. Jonathan Peter Parris
8. Elizabeth Helen Wiens & Ernest Frank Friesen
   - a. Jason Harlow Friesen & Jennifer Dawn Smith Jessup
     - i. Caden Jacob Riker Friesen ii. Laine Arwen E. Friesen
   - b. Trevor Julian Friesen & Jaime Nicole Powers
   - c. Erin Maria Leann Friesen
9. John Peter Wiens & Marjorie Helen Gorman
   - a. Michaela Joy Gorman Wiens
   - b. Peter James Gorman Wiens
10. Victor Peter Wiens & Elizabeth Jean Sanderson
    - a. Christopher Alan Merrill & Wendy Tesh
    - b. Sara Rae Merrill & James Phillip (J.P) Richie
      - Coleman James Alexander Richie   Mason Christopher Richie
    - c. Joseph Ryan Burke
    - d. Stuart Michel Burk
11. George Peter Wiens & Edith Lorraine Neumann (Harold Toews)
    - a. Ryan Kade Wiens & Michelle Angela Cameron
      - i. Mary Teresa (Tess) Cameron
    - b. Joel Lee Wiens
12. Naomi Ruth Wiens & Phillip James Kapplehoff
    - a. Kendra Renee Kapplehoff & John (Chip) Everett Heffelfinger
      - i. Ryan Everett Heffelfinger ii. Reagan Elizabeth Heffelfinger
    - b. Nadine Maria Kapplehoff
    - c. Rhome Gabriel Kapplehoff
13. Melita Margaret Wiens & Timothy Anthony Kudel
    - a. Leah Maria Kudel
    - b. Christina Lynn Kudel
    - c. Mark Alexander Kudel
14. Blondina Johanna Wiens & Russell Richard Funk
    - a. Matthew Lee Funk & Denica Leigh McLean
    - b. Mark Russell Funk

TABLE OF CONTENTS

Part Three - Obituaries   Page

Part Four - Appendix

PREFACE

A favorite toy of many children is the kaleidoscope. It is such a simple toy yet children are fascinated with its capabilities. Once you lift this toy to your eye and turn the tube at the very end, a myriad of colored glass, plastic and other objects constantly run into each other ever changing the design that is before you. Invented in 1816 by David Brewster, it was a popular toy during the Victorian age. Parents would give these toys to their children to encourage them to sit still in the parlor keeping them from becoming restless while their parents talked grown up talk.

In many ways the events of the twentieth century is like a kaleidoscope. It was always changing, always progressing forwards. A kaleidoscope has many different colors in it. Sometimes history would cast a rosy hue as it did in the 20's and 50's when everything seemed to be pointing to the American Dream. At other times the blending of colors would be drab or depressing as it was during the Great Depression.

This book is about the history of Canada and sometimes United States during the twentieth century. The term "American" is often used interchangeably with both the people of Canada and the United States; however the main focal point of the story is told from the prospective of one woman, Maria Martens and the people that influenced her life.This story is really told in two parts. The first part deals with the questions of what, where, when and how. I have tried to capture here the time period Maria Martens lived in and how it influenced the world at home and at large.

The second part deals with who she was, written from the viewpoint of her children and grandchildren. In this part, we have tried to capture the essence of what she meant to many people and how she and Peter Wiens directly influenced the lives that were entrusted into their care.

Prologue

The room is thick with anticipation. Standing room only, they say. The halls are decked with the finest décor that the kingdom has. Gabriel, the archangel stands at attention with his trumpet ready to sound upon a moments notice. It is the Coronation Day of the King. The day of anticipation has finally arrived. Everyone is dressed in their finest formal wear; shoes polished until they shine.

Suddenly the trumpets blast breaks the silence of anticipation. The Prince is on his way! Everyone turns their eyes in the direction of the sound of the horns ready to meet their soon-to-be King. But wait – the angel in charge needs to do the role call of the invited guests. His able assistant presents The Book – The Book with the names of all the invited guests. The angel receives The Book with reverence and care from his assistant and gently places it on a crystal clear stand.

He opens The Book and starts to call: Gerhard G. Derksen, Anna Derksen, Sara Derksen Wiebe; Peter P. Wiens, Gerhard Peter Wiens; Sadie Lyn Wiggins, Elizabeth Derksen Willems; Maria Georgina Martens – here!

The angelic choirs opens with joy and sings

When the trumpet of the Lord shall sound, and time shall be more,
And the morning breaks, eternal, bright and fair;
When the saved of earth shall gather over on the other shore,
And the roll is called up yonder, I'll be there.

On that bright and cloudless morning when the dead in Christ shall rise,
And the glory of His resurrection share;
When His chosen ones shall gather to their home beyond the skies,
And the role is called up yonder, I'll be there.

Let us labor for the Master from the dawn till setting sun,
Let us talk of all His wondrous love and care;
Then when all of life is over, and our work on earth is done,
And the roll is called up yonder, I'll be there.

After the roll call is completed, the guards open the back door. All voices hush as the Prince, garbed in rich purple velvety royal robes, walks up the aisle to the front. The guests are seated and the coronation proceeds. The crowned jewels are placed on the brow of His One and Only Son, Jesus. After the crown has been placed on the King, The Master turns toward the guests and announces, "Meet Your King!" The audience rises to their feet and breaks out with a thunderous applause unlike anything ever heard. With an awed reverence, they fall on their knees to worship Him.

***

What a wondrous day that will be when we see the coronation of Jesus as the King of Kings and Lord of Lords. As I was watching a recent episode of *Touched by an Angel*, one particular scene jumped out to me. The scenario was that of the crowning of Miss Colorado. There are a lot of contestants to choose from but one of the contestants, a latecomer, Tracy, has a dark secret that cannot be revealed. Monica, an angel, knows what the secret is and why Tracy is doing what she is doing. Tracy is a single parent who needs a lot of money for a very expensive operation for her son. While Tracy has her heart in the right place, she is doing it for all the wrong reasons.

Tracy has made it into the semifinals when Monica confronts her. Monica tells Tracy "Trust God to meet your need; don't trust money". Tracy snaps back in frustration, "God is a luxury I can't afford." Monica sadly but gently tells her that "God is a luxury you can't afford to live without". In the end Tracy has to decide whether to do what is right, taking a risk that could get her nothing. It took great courage for her to trust in Someone much greater than her.

***

This is the story of my Mother, Maria Derksen Wiens Martens. It is a story of faith, strength and great courage. Like Tracy, Maria was placed in a position many times over when she was forced to take risks without knowing the outcome. If Maria had dispensed with God out of her life, her story and our story would be so very different. But to Maria, God was not a luxury but at the very core of her surviving all the difficulties that entered her life.

During the course of her 89 years, she lived through the roaring 20's, the dirty 30's, two world wars, two marriages, single parenthood, self employment in her 50's and early 60's, and her golden retirement years. To her, God was not a luxury but a necessity that she couldn't live without. Her very soul depended on the faithfulness of His character.

PART 1

Retrospectives

Chapter 1

"God blessed us with a little daughter"

Her parents, Gerhard and Anna Derksen, named this baby girl "Maria Georgina Derksen" and these seven words were written in the diary of Gerhard G. Derksen shortly after the birth of this very precious tiny babe. This comment found in her father's diary made Maria, their 9th daughter, feel very secure and loved in her parents' home. The name given to a child is special and usually has a special meaning. Maria means 'the perfect one' and Georgina, the feminine version of 'George' means 'farmer' – hence Maria Georgina – 'the perfect farmer'.

The day was Thursday, November 2, 1911. The weather was very cold and winter had arrived early that year in Borden, Saskatchewan. In fact, it came so early that farmers were unable to harvest their crops. The temperature was a very cold minus 14 degrees Celsius (6 degrees Fahrenheit) with a blizzard blowing outside.

According to Gerhard's diary, on the day of her birth Maria's father had hauled 14 loads of sheaves to be threshed later.

The birth of this child was extra special and extra personal because this baby girl became my Mother and a major influence in my life.

MARIA'S PARENTAGE

Maria's Father

Gerhard G. Derksen, the third of seven children, was born in Russia in the colony of Molotschna in the village of Rudnerweide. His parents, Gerhard P. Derksen (March 1, 1836-1920) and Anna Andreas Pankratz (May 14, 1842-1920) were married on December 3, 1859. Gerhard Jr. had an older brother, Henry, and an older sister, Elizabeth. He had also had four other brothers whose names are not known.

Gerhard and Anna were poor, and made their living renting land from others with the intent of someday having their own land. However, they lost everything they saved due to failed crops so Gerhard also worked as a salesman and was able to save 500 Rubles, which was pretty good but not quite enough for property. Eventually, they did get their land when lots were cast in Sagradoffka, a village of the Motolshna colony, and eleven landless farmers including Gerhard P. Derksen were fortunate enough to be granted a piece of land.

During the move to their new home, six year old Gerhard decided that he could do just about anything that his brother Henry could do – this included herding the cattle on the ten day journey. With great reluctance his mother agreed and let him go. But he did not count on how difficult the work of herding cattle was, or how quickly he would get tired. With no one to pay any attention to his pitiful crying he had no choice but to continue on until the wagons caught up with them. This experience taught him just how much his mother cared for him.

After the family built a large Mennonite house, they started a school for the children – right in the front room of the Derksen home until such time as a schoolhouse was built. Initially their teachers were mostly neighbors who did not have much education themselves. Mostly they planned to teach the children readin' and ritin' and 'rithemetic, the basic essentials of that day. Teachers were hard to keep. They had little learning themselves or they couldn't agree with the philosophy of the parents, which sometimes caused them to be fired. Books were scarce. Consequently, he did not learn much in the first three years of his education. He read mostly out of catechism books that were used to prepare an individual for church membership. When he got older, Gerhard and his brother, Henry, went to a private school held in the home of Mr. Koehn. Gerhard was behind in his studies so his teacher tried to teach him mostly by pounding the information into his head, with a book or with his hand two or three times a day. Afraid to report this behavior to his parents, the abuse continued for three months until his brother Henry came to the rescue. From that time on, he attended the village school until the end of that particular school year. This was a relief for him, as he did not enjoy going to school.

Gerhard's youth could be best described as 'wild' and 'shameful' with an unwillingness to listen to the urging of the Holy Spirit. His image of a Christian was a person who wore a 'long face'. He wanted to be happy and live as he pleased. On the other hand, his parents wanted Gerhard to grow up, be baptized, and join the church at the age of 18. They wanted him to become a Christian and live a decent life. The companionship of the worldly young men Gerhard chose to keep company with and his new indulgence of smoking tobacco made it difficult for him to comply with his parents' wishes. However, they were his parents, and one needed to obey his parents, so Gerhard agreed to join the church. He began the catechism classes necessary in preparation for this very important step that would make him a Christian. The knowledge gleaned from these classes was good for his soul, but there was no repentance or confession in this group of 80 boys. He did, however, agree to stop seeing his worldly friends and stop smoking tobacco.

By now he was under the conviction of the Holy Spirit and for the first time, he listened to the Holy Spirit by not going through with the baptism. He thought that Christians had to be perfect, and he was not able to be perfect – even though he kept his promise to stop smoking tobacco and leave his worldly friends. His life if anything got worse not better.

At the age of 21, in lieu of joining the military, all Mennonite boys had to serve 4 years in the forestry service. Still under the conviction of the Holy Spirit, Gerhard started his term of service in 1888. Life in the camp at Ratzina was rough but the food and clothing were better than what his family could afford at home. Gerhard described his life at this time as still very wild, and his life had not improved any but rather it had gone further downhill. Realizing that he could never attain perfection in his life on earth, he was once again tempted to conform to the church and become baptized without any repentance. Gerhard noticed that baptism and church membership had not changed any of his friends' lives. Again he resisted the temptation to follow through with this important act.

During Gerhard's first year of service, his father became a believer and accepted Christ as his Savior. During his first furlough at home his father spoke to him of spiritual matters with much earnestness, and the Holy Spirit started to work again in his heart. During Gerhard's second year in the forest service, his mother was also saved and both of his parents were baptized. During his last two years away from home, four other brothers had joined their parents in their faith. By now, Gerhard began to go to a place of solitude and pray for peace but he never found it.

On his second leave he found a completely different atmosphere in his parents' home. They had devotions and were happier people all around. Though he wanted to be saved, he thought he wasn't good enough. Nevertheless, he attended Bible studies and prayer meetings. He was under much conviction and finally one night he broke down and asked the Lord to forgive his sins, but he had a lot of difficulty accepting the forgiveness that was offered. He didn't see or have any hope for his salvation. Oh, how he struggled with all of this turmoil. During this time, they sang a song "Suser Heiland, deine Gnade ist viel grosser als man denkt", which translated into English means "Precious Savior, your grace is much greater than we think". These words broke through the thick veil that kept him from accepting this forgiveness. He finally believed and accepted the Christ who died on the cross for his sins.

Despite the cold weather, he followed the Lord in baptism on Christmas Day in December of 1889. His recording of this event stated that he, like the Eunuch of old in Acts, went on his way rejoicing. He never regretted the decision that he made that winter. Throughout his 66 years of life he consistently told people of the Christ who died for him. After his death in 1933 some of his grandchildren remember the spiritual life that he lived.

Maria's Mother

Anna Pankratz was born to John Andrew Pankratz and Justina Klassen Pankratz in Sagradoffka, Russia. Her father, John Pankratz, was born on June 19 of 1840. John's father, Andrew Pankratz, died when John was 14 or 15 years old. Because his mother (whose name is not known) was very poor he worked away from home as a hired man until 1865 when, at 25 years old, he married 18-year-old Justina Klassen.

Justina Klassen was born on July 20 of 1844. When she was 9 years old she was loaned out to the Dyck family, but records do not state the reason for this loan. It was intended to be for a few weeks but lasted for nine years, until her marriage to John Pankratz. One and a half years into their marriage, John & Justina Pankratz moved to Furstenlande, Nickolofelt. Here they lost three children – one as an infant, one at four years old, and a three-year son who drowned. Then they lived in Alexandrathal in the Molotshna Colony before they moved to Sagradoffka when Anna was 8 years old. Here they had four more children, Henry (1877), John (1881), Justina (1883), and David (1886).

The Bible was one of the subjects taught in Anna's school, and she regarded it with much joy during her lifetime. On July 20, 1886, her Mother Justina's 42ⁿᵈ Birthday, they were baptized and became members of the Tiege Mennonite Brethren Church (M.B.) in Sagradovka. I will let Anna Pankratz Derksen tell the story of how she was saved in her own words:

"As I was fourteen years old the Lord led it so that two preacher brethren came to our village. One was brother Klassen and the other Gerhard Siemens who received permission to have evening services in the village school. In our village there were only a few saved people but the Lord gave grace that a revival came about. My parents also got saved and as the brethren visited them they read God's word and prayed together.

Brother Gerhard Siemens came to me in the room where I was and he asked me whether I wanted to be saved. That was my deep desire and he talked to me, showed me the way to salvation after which we prayed together (but I have also often prayed alone). I received forgiveness of my sins through the blood of the Lamb and I was baptized in the summer 1886, by Jacob Richert, the grandfather of Frank Peters (Tina Derksen's husband) and I was accepted in the Tiege Mennonite Brethren church.

After I was baptized I came into a deep depression. I could not believe that I was saved. It seemed as though I had never been saved, all this seemed like a delusion and I felt I did not have enough experience – I was so unhappy. I prayed a lot and the Lord heard my prayer and gave me light again and has kept me from a life of doubts."

One song that reflects what Anna was feeling is "Blessed Assurance". In 1873, Phoebe Knaff played a tune for Fanny Crosby and asked her what she thought it said. Within minutes, Fanny wrote the words of the well-known hymn that we know as "Blessed Assurance". Read the words below and see for yourself the story of salvation in this song.

1. *Blessed Assurance, Jesus is mine!*
   O what a foretaste of Glory divine!
   Heir of salvation, purchase of God,
   Born of His Spirit, washed in His blood.

2. *Perfect submission, perfect delight,*
   Visions of rapture now burst on my sight;
   Angels descending, bring from above
   Echoes of mercy, whispers of love.

3. *Perfect submission, all is at rest,*
   I in my Savior am happy and blest;
   Watching and waiting, looking above,
   Filled with His goodness, lost in His love.

Chorus:
   This is my story, this is my song,
   Praising my Savior all the day long;
   This is my story, this is my song;
   Praising my Savior all the day long.

Maria's Parents' Life Together

During Gerhard's third leave from the Forestry service he went to visit to his brother, Henry, in Sagradoffka and there he met his beloved Anna Pankratz. This time when he went back to Ratzina it was more difficult to say his farewells. During that time period, parents had the right to censor letters between a daughter and her beau, so they were unable to express in writing how they felt about each other. On top of that he had an accident that cut his right hand (his writing hand) half off which prevented him from communicating with Anna. During this time of difficulty, she went through much suffering based on the rumors she had been told regarding the accident.

Despite these hurdles, Gerhard and Anna celebrated their engagement on November 20 of 1891. They were married two weeks later on December 10 in Anna's home. After their marriage, they moved to Domishen Kosaken where Gerhard's parents had moved a year or so earlier. They lived with his parents for a year until they got some land of their own. It was during their stay with his parents that their oldest son, George, was born.

They struggled much during the 13 years they lived in Russia – first from poor crops, then from Gerhard's severe asthma that lasted for 6 years during which time the Derksens prayed for healing. After promising the Lord that he would give 100 Rubles to a mission if he was healed, the Lord healed Gerhard. A man of great integrity, he kept his promise.

Gerhard and Anna's last farm in Russia was in Hamburg, in the Molotshna Colony. He farmed this property for 2 years. Barely able to support their family after more poor crops, he and Anna sold their property. Already deep in debt, they decided to start over in Canada. Together with 8 children ranging from 2 months up to 13 years, they said their final earthly farewells to their families and left for North America on May 23, 1905. They left Russia by train, and then sailed from Germany on June 17 on the *Bremen*. They docked in New York City on June 27, under the welcoming light of Lady Liberty.

From New York City Anna, Gerhard, and their brood of 8 children traveled by train to Montreal and finally to Saskatchewan, "the land of plenty", settling in the Great Deer, Sask. area. They arrived in Rosthern sometime in July of 1905.
Here they were welcomed to the area by Gerhard's sister and her husband (Elizabeth and Daniel Thiessen) who had immigrated two years earlier. They stayed with Elizabeth and Daniel until they found land of their own in Borden.

During the years that Anna lived in Borden, more sorrow came to her family. Her daughter Sara died in 1930 at 30 years of age, followed by the death of Anna's husband Gerhard. After the marriage of her youngest son, Henry, she lived with several of her children moving from place to place until she settled into the home of Jake and Agnes Stobbe where she lived for 20 years. Her final years were spent in a nursing home until her death at 98 years of age on October 18, 1969. Her mind was clear and sharp to the very end. Despite the fact that there were 80 grandchildren, she knew each and every one of them. While it may seem that Anna had a sorrowful life both in Russia and Canada, she led an active life. However, she regretted that she never learned to live by herself when she was able to do so. Her life – regrets and all – was not a wasted one. She encouraged her children's gifts. Each child had a different talent – Maria played the piano, Margaret had a good voice and so on. Anna raised her children to be hard workers who in turn passed this trait down to their children.

Anna knew how to plan the order of her day well. Each child was given responsibilities. The oldest boy and girl at home were designated as the second in command. This meant that the younger siblings had to respect and obey their authority. Hard work was not new to Anna. For example, Anna made the down for the feather pillows the family slept on. While the geese were still alive, Anna would hold a goose upside down or place it on her lap and pluck some of the down off the goose's breast. These down feathers in turn contributed to the pillow stuffing.

Anna and Gerhard lived Godly lives and taught their children and grandchildren how to love the Lord by example. Many of her grandchildren became pastors or missionaries while others became well-respected members in their churches and chosen vocations. To the grandchildren who lived close by, she and her husband were special people. Christmas was always a special time in their home. As the family increased in size, Christmas was divided into two days. Christmas Day was reserved for the aunts and the uncles plus the younger children while the older children would arrive on New Years Day for their special time with the grandparents. One grandchild described Christmas as a day of singing Christmas carols plus choruses they had learned followed by recitations of things they had memorized. Following this Grandma Anna would disappear and bring out big bags of peanuts. The grandchildren played many games while visiting the grandparents. Those Sundays with the grandparents were very special. She always had a treat for a visiting grandchild in her writing desk. During the course of the year, if there were enough children present, they had enough people to play ball especially when the Rempel-Block family came over.

For a period of time, she lived with daughter, Anna Block, and her family. One member of the family described her as a busy woman who did whatever she could to contribute to the household. She was never a guest but rather was treated as a member of the family. She'd sit in her rocking chair and knit stockings or mittens for the children. She encouraged her grandchildren in their schoolwork and influenced their Christian life. Perhaps the best word picture painted of Grandma Anna was that written by Sarah, another grandchild. Grandma Anna was living with her daughter, Anna Block, (Sarah's mother) at this time. Grandma Anna was a woman who loved her Lord very much and lived what she believed leading by example.

If one went past her half-opened door, they would often find her in her rocking chair holding her "Precious" Bible in her hands on her lap reading God's word. Her face was often one of prayerful meditation. She would pray for each of her grandchildren wherever they were. She encouraged her grandchildren in what endeavor they chose to take – even supporting those that went out as missionaries as one grandchild recalls.

When one of the grandchildren gave into the temptation of taking some candy from her drawer, she was quick to forgive the little offender giving the child a warm and tender embrace that warmed the soul.

She made sure to have a quiet time of devotions with the adult children that she lived with each day. This was a high point of her day – each adult encouraging and instructing the other. Another grandchild recalls that she enjoyed nothing better than to be asked about her pioneering days. It seems she had an intuition about where each of her children, grandchildren, and great grandchildren were spiritually.

Another grandchild, Esther, recalled a few of her grandmother's character traits. She described her as a woman who honored and glorified God. She had a listening ear, a firm restraint on evil, a forgiving spirit, yet she was also respectful, hospitable, compassionate, and easy to get along with.

On one occasion, Esther was in the gooseberry patch. All but one of the bushes had been picked. As the girl started to pick some of the berries off the bush, she was attacked by a swarm of wasps. Her grandmother was compassionate toward Esther helping her as best she could.

Grandma Anna was also interested in everything that went on outside. She'd walk from the house to various parts of the farm and watch what was going on or assist the grandchildren in some of their chores such as picking fruit from the garden.

At the time of her death, she had already lost a number of her own children but she had been blessed with 80 grandchildren – many of whom were married with families of their totaling 187 great grand children and two great great grandchildren. She was the last charter member of the original Borden M. B. church to be buried.

The Fate of Anna's family in Russia after 1905

After the death of Anna's mother, Justina, on April 30, 1900 her father married Margaret Giesbrecht (who died in 1937). John and Margaret had a son named Peter in 1904. Records show that John and Margaret also adopted a girl named Margaret who married Anna's brother David.

Not much is known about the relatives born to this family except that they suffered greatly - losing everything they had when they had to flee for their lives. Communism had taken over and the political situation was extremely difficult. Those who chose not to cooperate with the system suffered the consequences.

Records indicate that Anna's brother, Peter, married a girl named Mary. Peter took care of Mother Margaret until her death in 1937. In November of that same year, Peter was taken away and was never heard from again. At the time of Peter's disappearance, Mary was pregnant with her second child. During the pregnancy, Mary's relatives came to see her and took Mary's son Henry with them for a weeklong visit. Sadly, the train they traveled on was bombed and all the travelers were killed. She gave birth to a daughter named Betty in June of 1938. Of all of Anna's family, only Mary and her daughter Betty came to Canada where Mary's brothers lived.

The future of the other members of her family remained a mystery though her records indicated that John and Peter were believers. We do know that Anna's brothers John, David, and Henry and their families were forced to flee for their lives and experienced much hunger. Of the three brothers, only the fate of Anna's brother David is known. Anna records that he was killed when a wall fell on him.

A View of Canada in 1911

In 1911, Canadian Federal elections were held. In Canada, Federal Elections can be called at any time. If one party thinks they have the upper edge over the prevailing party they may call one and that is what Conservative Party leader Sir Robert Laird Borden did in 1911, and the result was the defeat of the Liberal Party.

The main issue at hand was Unrestricted Reciprocity, or mutual exchange with the United States. Sir Wilfrid Laurier, the Liberal Party Leader for approximately 18 years, was in favor of lowering the tariff with United States but Borden was not. In late January, Laurier and his Liberal government succeeded in negotiating a free trade agreement for natural products and a short list of manufactured goods with the United States. Borden seized this as an opportunity for the new nation of Canada to rise up and declare their Canadian nationalism with their strong ties to Mother Britain.

At this time more than half of Canada's exports went to Britain, but on the other hand they imported nearly 60% of their goods from the United States. In short, they received more goods from the United States (60%) than they sent to their neighbor to the south (40%). By definition "An ideal trade" connection is when foreign countries import more from your country than you import from them.[1]

Borden, waving the British flag and beating on a patriotic drum, told Canadian voters that they had to choose between the Spirit of Canadianism and the Spirit of Continentalism. He argued that if they continued with free trade, Canada would be Americanized and their British heritage would be destroyed. Laurier argued that free trade was simply a good economic move for Canada. The voters swayed toward Borden and Canadianism, thus defeating the Liberal party.

Either way, Laurier found himself in a catch 22 position – on one hand, in Quebec he was viewed as an imperialistic traitor to the French because of his involvement of the Canadian army in the Boer war. On the other hand, he was seen in Ontario as an anti-imperialistic traitor to the English.

The other issue in this election was the Naval Service Bill that Laurier introduced in 1910. The purpose of this bill was to make Canada less dependent on Britain and British imperialism. When the Boer War broke out, Laurier had hoped to unite French and English Canada into a unique unit of Canadian nationalism rather than remain unquestionably loyal to Britain.

During the Boer War, Britain automatically assumed that Canada would send military support to fight the war in South Africa. English Canada supported the war but French Canada opposed the very idea of supporting Britain's 'imperialist wars'. French speaking Quebec politicians like Henri Bourassa and Laurie supported the idea of a united independent Canada but Bourassa opposed Laurier when Laurier allowed a volunteer force to fight in the war even though the only other option was to call up an official army.

About this time the Naval Service Bill was introduced, Bourassa was of the conviction that the British would call on the Canadian Navy whenever they needed it just as they did with the Canadian Army. On the other hand, Pro-British imperialists also opposed Laurier's attempt to remove Canada from the Empire. So it is that the Navel Service Bill and the Reciprocity Treaty of 1911 led to the downfall of the Liberal government. This was Canadian politics in 1911.

Maria's Parents

Gerhard and Anna (Pankratz) Derksen

1924

Maria's Grandparents

Andrew and Justina (Klassen) Pankratz

Russian believers take their confession of faith very seriously, even in the dead of winter when bodies of water are frozen over solidly. When Gerhard G. Derksen was baptized on Christmas Day, a hole was cut in the ice similar to this picture for the occasion. *photo courtesy of Bob Merrill, CMA missionary to Russia*

It was common for babies to be born at home in the early 1900's. This is the Birthplace of Maria as it was seen in 1909 before the birth of Aunt Ella.

Chapter 2

The Origin of the Russian Mennonite Brethren Church

Menno Simon's Influence in the Mennonite Movement

The birth of the Mennonite Brethren Church was not without difficulty, receiving opposition from both the established church and civil authorities. Menno Simons (ca 1496 – ca 1561), a Roman Catholic priest, gave up his priesthood in 1536 and embraced the views of a group known as the Anabaptists in the Netherlands. They preferred to be called the 'brethren' to avoid the stigma of the name 'Anabaptist'. Only after his death did they become known by the name of 'Mennonites'. They were granted freedom of religion in 1676.

The Mennonites did, however, share some common doctrinal beliefs with the Anabaptists such as:
1. The authority of the Bible as the final and infallible rule for faith and practice.
2. The church was to be a group of regenerated (born again) believers in contrast to the state church who believed membership made one a Christian in the sense of being born again.
3. Baptism was done by immersion.
4. They opposed infant baptism.

A Brief History of the Early Mennonites in Russia

In 1771-1773 Catherine II, the German wife of Peter III, gave an invitation to the Germans and other Europeans to settle in the area vacated by the defeated Turks in Southern Russia. She wanted good farmers for these lands and invited persecuted people of all faiths to come. Despite this invitation being issued, the Mennonites did not migrate to southern Russia until the 1780's. Many decided to go because of the political climate during that time. The French Revolution had failed and increasing military preparations in Prussia made the Mennonites nervous. They were non-resistant by nature but some of the government taxes (which were based on land ownership) went directly to support both the military and the church. Although the Mennonites felt that they should pay their fair share of the taxes, they did not support either of the areas where their money was going. This state of affairs prompted many to respond to the invitation of Catherine II and relocate in Southern Russia where she promised them exemption from the military.

For the Mennonites who chose to stay behind, this created a major problem. They did not give up their position without a struggle. The more land the Mennonites owned, the more money the government lost that could have been contributed to the support of state functions. To keep them from gaining more land, the government slapped controls on the Mennonites. These restrictions put young couples desiring to start their homes into a state of being landless. It has been said that a Mennonite without a farm is like a horse without a rider. The only recourse they had was to migrate.

Following the enactment of the Prussian universal military training law in 1814, the Mennonites appealed for an exemption. They were granted this appeal on one condition – which was that they pay a heavy tax in addition to the support that they had to pay to the military academy. By 1868 the nonresistance influence that governed the Mennonites was losing its hold. By the time WWI broke out, most of the Mennonites from Prussia in the army were in regular service positions.

The first group that came from Prussia consisted of eight families and totaled about 50 people. They took their nonresistance position very seriously and saw the invitation of Catherine II as a way out of Prussia. It took them five weeks to travel less than 300 miles from Danzig (now renamed Gdansk, Poland) to reach Riga (now the capital of Latvian). With a month off to rest their horses, it took them another six weeks to travel the next 300 miles to reach Dubrovna (see Map 3 and 4). They were forced to winter at Dubrovna because Russia was at war with Turkey. By the following year when they were free to travel, there were some 228 families in their camp waiting to go further.

Oddly enough, in this first group there was not a single minister. To complicate this obstacle further, there were also twelve couples who desired to be married. An offering was taken to send someone back to Danzig with a petition to send them a minister. The Danzig church replied by telling them they should conduct their own elections for a minister. Of the twelve names given to Danzig, four were approved (of which Bernhard Penner was one) and commissioned by letter to serve as elders.

The first colony at Chortiza consisted of 400 families on the Dnieper River in the Ukraine. Living conditions, to say the least, were difficult for these first pioneers. They lived in mud huts that became even muddier in the rain. They also experienced material loss. Their horses were either stolen or lost due to the lack of fences. Their lumber was of inferior quality and the families were dirt poor. Disease and death also took its toll.

Coming into Russia they were granted special concessions in 1788 enabling them to control their own religious, educational and civic concerns pretty much as they had done in Prussia. They were also granted complete freedom of religion and exemption from serving in the military for 100 years. When one colony ran out of land, daughter colonies were established in new areas.

They did not receive the financial aid promised them for up to eight years. In addition to the lack of funds, they were also experiencing discord and strife in their camps. These were just a few of the problems they experienced. Despite these obstacles, by the early 1800's, these 400 families were established in fifteen villages farming about 89,100 acres of land

Map 1

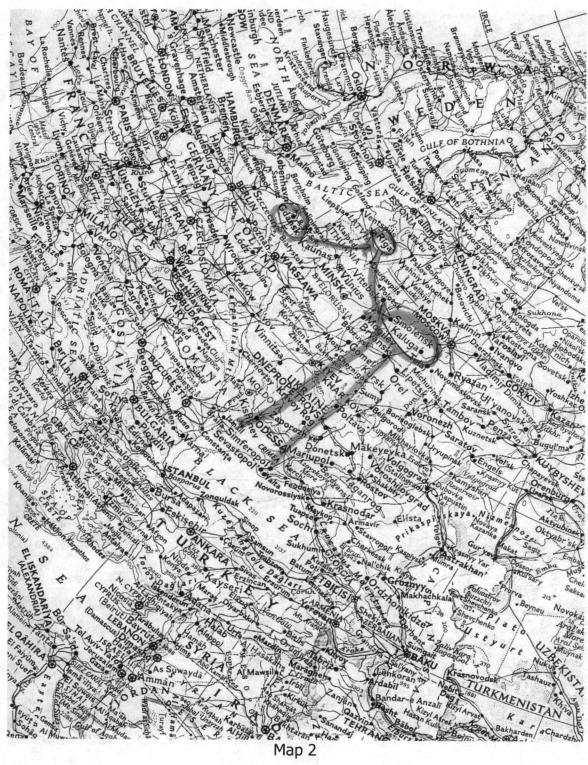

Map 2

The Birth of the Russian Mennonite Brethren Church

    The Mennonite Brethren Church itself was born on January 6, 1860. A pietist named Eduard Wust of Lutheran background conducted meetings among the Mennonites in Molotshna stressing repentance and conversion leading many Mennonites into a personal relationship with Jesus Christ. He led them, whenever possible, in Bible studies and prayer cells. Though unrelated at first, this revival started first in the Molotschna colony and spread to the Chortitza colony.

    Pietism was a reform movement in Lutheran circles that stressed personal religious feelings. Evangelical in nature, they had a profound effect on 17th and 18th century Christianity in Europe. They stressed personal internal religious experiences rather than outward conformity to the church dogma and practice. They believed in the rebirth of mankind in Christ and regarded the church sacraments as symbols rather than the means of grace. Another challenge they faced was trying to bring renewal among their own people who had become apathetic in spiritual matters. They became discouraged by their fellow Mennonites' lack of interest and were accused by the mother church of being unspiritual. This led to the estrangement and separation between the Mennonites and the newly formed Mennonite Brethren. Finally they chose to interpret the scriptures for themselves rather than solely depending on the clergy to do this for them.

    One of the touchy issues was the matter of communion. Under the dictates of the Mennonites, communion was to be administered only by the church elders and not by lay people. In 1859 under the direction of Abraham Cornelson, a schoolteacher, a private communion was held with none of the church elders present. Disciplined by the elders, the Brethren agreed never to do such an irregular thing again promising obedience to all things not contrary to their conscience and the Word of God. The elders worked toward reconciliation but the Brethren as they were known (they addressed each other as 'Brother') felt they could no longer fellowship with the membership of the mother church.

    At a private meeting on January 6, 1860, Abraham Cornelson put a document before those present, fully aware that if they signed it they could face persecution since it was calling for a formal separation from the Mennonite church. It charged the Mennonite church with growing corruption and its leaders for allowing their spiritual condition to decay. The Brethren were in agreement with their basic doctrines, but it was the church's decline in spiritual matters that were their main concern. Eighteen people signed this document that day, and nine others signed it a day or so later.

    The church elders denied these charges and placed this matter in the hands of the colony's civil authorities. They wanted the Brethren to 'see the error of their way' and be returned to the church by force. Colony administration asked the Brethren for an explanation. They responded on January 23rd stating they would have gladly remained in the church if their ministers were obedient to the Word of God, but since they weren't they had no choice but to leave. They also firmly stated that it was their intent to remain Mennonites.

Under the Penal Code of 1857, the administrators treated them as a secret society and all meetings not sponsored by the established church were forbidden. Abraham Cornelson, a father with a large family, was banished to live among a nomadic people for a time. Others were ruined economically with legal travel documents being denied them. Thus they became prisoners in their colony. They were not allowed to leave and officials made their staying unbearable.

The Mennonite Brethren (M.B.) group fought for government recognition, which in turn would also force the church to recognize them. On the other hand, if they failed they could lose their special privileges. Government officials were friendly and helpful to them in their contact with the Baptists.

The church at Molotschna was given two options by the colony authorities: expel the Brethren or grant them recognition. Refusing to accept this civic action of the church, the Brethren sent a petition to the Czar in the spring of 1862 to do something on their behalf. In October of 1862, the General Conference agreed to accept them on the condition that the confession of their faith was the same as theirs.

In an attempt to suppress the Brethren movement and hoping that the church would set the wheels in motion for expulsion, the colony administrators in 1863 ordered the village officials not to recognize marriages performed by the Brethren and to record all births in the name of the mother treating them as illegitimate.

The government answered their petition on this latest uproar on March 5, 1864 by formally recognizing them as Mennonite Brethren in the full sense of the word. Despite the division between the two groups, the two churches started to work together on matters of common interest. This was the church that the Wiens-Pauls family grew up in.

Chapter 3

The Establishment of the Borden M.B. Church

A 1901 census reveals that there were 3,683 Mennonites in the Rosthern area. By 1911 that number had increased to 8,000. Mennonites came to Saskatchewan for several reasons. Land was becoming scarce in Russia, the Russian government was beginning to break some of the promises they had made to the Mennonites, and finally the Canadian Dominion Land Act of 1872 made 160 acres of land available to every immigrant for a registration fee of only ten dollars. After working the land for three years, that land became theirs providing they met certain requirements. It was just too good an opportunity to ignore.

It is a fact that wherever the Mennonites moved a church would be established, and it was no different with the group of Mennonites moving to the Borden area. Between 1902 and 1903 a group of Mennonites from Russia settled in the Borden area hoping to gain from the opportunity of getting 160 acres of land as a homestead. They were fortunate to have a spiritual leader in their group by the name of David Klassen (grandfather of Hulda Klassen who later married Maria's youngest brother, Henry G. Derksen). Although they were not officially organized until 1906, they began to meet in 1903. At first they met in homes. Later on when the Hoffnungsfeld School was built, the meetings were moved to the Hoffnungsfeld "Field of Hope" School as a central meeting place, but Mid-week services were still held in homes. In 1907 they constructed their first church building on two acres donated by one of their elders, David Dyck. This church was used until 1952 when a new building was erected. What was first known as the Hoffnungsfeld Mennonite Brethren Church ultimately became known as the Borden M. B. Church.

Right from the start, the leaders of the church stressed the importance of church life and a personal commitment to Jesus Christ. Everything else flowed out from this. It was believed that a healthy church had a mission outreach, and some of their missions were to support the Russian ministry in Blaine Lake as well as teaching Sunday school to those who lived in marginal areas.

Lay ministers led the church until 1965 when they began to have paid pastors. The structure of the church was designed to seat women on one side and the men on the other. The main part of the building was heated with a wood pot bellied stove, and there was another stove in the nursery. The Sunday school was segregated – girls and women were taught separately from the men and boys, and this policy did not change until much later in the 1960's. Gerhard Derksen was one of the founding teachers, instructing the older married men. He was also very active in the church serving as a deacon as well as a treasurer. In the beginning, church meetings were held in various homes and often in the Derksen home. He and Anna were described as godly, devoted Christians who took their children to church and Sunday school.

One of the areas where Gerhard had great influence on his family was missions. He served on the M.B. Foreign Mission Board from the beginning of his early years in Canada, often housing the missionaries and traveling preachers that came through the area. He also managed the finances for the City Missions for a long period of time. Through all of this activity he had the support of his wife. Gerhard and Anna loved to sing. They took their faith seriously. They would lead their family in devotions both morning and night. Daughter Susie recalled that they were a blessing to their children.

The original Borden M.B. Church

This church was later torn down in 1952

Chapter 4

Early Growing Up Years

In order to understand the character and personality of Maria, we need to go back and examine the Derksen home in general. Different relatives described Gerhard and Anna as strict. Although they were hardworking people, they did not tolerate laziness or put up with disobedience.

Five children (Tina, Ella, Maria, Henry and Susie) were born to the Derksen family in Canada. At the time of Maria's birth the family was already considered to be quite large. Her oldest brother, George, was already 18 years old and the youngest child, Ella, was 2 years old. They joined the older children who had emigrated from Russia (Gerhard, Justina, Anna, John, Sara, Elizabeth, Margaret and Agnes). Eventually two more children, Henry and Susie would join the family. In 1915 the total size of the family consisted of 10 daughters and 3 sons.

Anna & Gerhard established a unique sense of responsibility. In the Derksen home there were two levels of authority. In the absence of any parents, the younger children would adhere to the authority of whichever brother and sister pair was the oldest still living at home at the time. They were taught to respect this order of discipline.

Life at home was not all work; there was fun as well. Before Maria turned two years old, another chapter started in the Derksen family. Her oldest sister, Justina, married a young farmer named Peter Bergman. This was the first wedding to happen. As the older children married they added more little faces to the family circle. When these nieces and nephews came over to visit Grandma Anna and Grandpa Gerhard they became playmates for the youngest Aunts and Uncle. One niece, Esther Bergman, was an only child for many years. She told me once that she didn't come so much to see Grandma and Grandpa but to play with her aunts and uncle. By the time the last daughter, Susie, was born in December of 1915, George, Anna and Justina were married and two of them had already started their families. A third grandchild was born two months after the youngest Derksen child was born. Thus it was that nieces and nephews played right alongside with the youngest of the aunts and one uncle. They played with paper dolls and baby dolls as well as physical sports such as 'horsie'. To play 'horsie', someone would be the driver and two or more others would be the horses. Sometimes when Maria was one of the 'horses', they would try to run away from the driver.

Sundays were special – the highlight of the week. The Derksen household would often have thirty to forty people over for lunch. Sometimes they would get the 'old' men to run races with them, and sometimes they would play indoor games and sing for a couple of hours at a time. Of course, having this many people over for dinner had its downside as well, especially when it came to eating. The custom of the home was that the men (grandpa, his sons and sons-in-law) were fed first followed by the women, and finally the children who must have been very hungry by this time.

The Derksen family was one with many talents. Some of the older sisters, such as Margaret, were gifted with beautiful voices. During the course of her growing up years, Maria developed a gift for playing the piano – a talent she used her entire life wherever she lived. To encourage her skill, her parents scraped together enough money to purchase a piano for Maria. She was a self-taught pianist and in her teens played for the Borden church choir. Prior to her marriage in 1934 she gave her future sister-in-law, Hulda Klassen, piano lessons. Sister Susie also learned to play the piano. After Maria's marriage, Hulda and later Susie played the organ for the church. Maria played all the way until the end of her life.

Church was seen in both a social as well as a spiritual context. Sunday school was very important along with the memorization of scripture verses. The church founders stressed the importance of preparing themselves by doing their homework for Sunday school as well as bringing their Bibles with them. In her writing, Maria recalled that she did not even attend Sunday school until she was five years old. She did not as yet own a winter coat and remembered being enfolded in her father's big wrap-around sheepskin coat that was big enough for the both of them. What a feeling of warmth and comfort that must have been on a cold winter day.

The Mennonites spoke German. Their church services were done in High German, which was formal and considered the real language of the Germans. However at home the mother tongue was Low German, which is considered a dialect. To prepare children for the understanding and speaking of the High German language they received half an hour of High German instruction each day at school.

How can one talk about the church without mentioning the events of Christmas? Parents would donate a sum of money or products for the occasion. Those bags must have been a welcome presence in the home – especially the poorer homes.

Maria's Early Education

In 1905, when the Derksen family arrived in Saskatchewan, there was much work to be done in setting up a home and breaking the land for seeding the following year. Therefore, the Hoffnungsfeld School was constructed in 1906. Because of all the help that was needed at home, many of the older Derksen children were not able to attend school regularly. Even her sister Tina who had ambitions to be a nurse had to drop out of school to help the family at home. Ella was the first child to finish Grade Eight. Maria attended the King George School along with her sisters Ella and Susie and younger brother Henry.

School was very different in 1916. The King George School was a one-room school that housed all the students through 8th grade. Classrooms were heated by the potbelly stove situated in the center to keep everyone warm. Electricity did not exist. Each school day was opened with the Lord's Prayer and a Bible reading. Most of the children came to school from homes that spoke only German and they learned to read and write English in school since English was the spoken language in the Borden area schools with the exception of a half hour of instruction in the High German language.

In the Borden area schools, students were sent outside for their physical education. They played games such as softball in the warm weather. In the winter they erected a high pile of snow and iced it down with water. Once it was iced down real good, it was ready for sliding down. The only permanent playground equipment was a two-seater swing and a seesaw.

All of the grade levels were taught the 3 R's – readin' (reading), 'ritin' (writing) and 'rithmetic (arithmetic) as well as geography, spelling, and penmanship with a strong emphasis placed on penmanship. In singing class, they learned a new song each week. One of Maria's favorites was "*Old Black Joe*".

Old Black Joe was written in 1861 by Stephen Foster, a musician who also wrote other classics as *De Camptown Races, Old Folks at Home, Jeannie with the Light Brown Hair,* and *Dixie.* It is about a man named Joe who has seen his friends from the past die one by one. Now an old man, he is remembering those good ole days and reacting to those feelings of being left behind. Here are some of the lyrics of the song that Maria used to sing:

Gone are the days
When my heart was young and gay.
Gone are my friends
From the cotton fields away.
Gone from this place,
To a better land I know.
I hear their gentle voices calling:
Old Black Joe.

Why do I weep
When my heart should feel no pain
Why do I sigh
That my friends come not again
Grieving for forms
Now departed long ago
I hear their gentle voices calling:
Old Black Joe.

Where are the hearts
Once so happy and so free
The children so dear
That I held upon my knee
Gone to the shore
Where my soul has longed to go
I hear their gentle voices calling:
Old Black Joe.
Chorus:

I'm coming, I'm coming
For my head is bending low
I hear their gentle voices calling
Old Black Joe.

Maria loved going to school and when she completed 8th grade she desired to go to high school. However there were no school buses in existence to take farm children from their homes to the high school in the village of Borden. In order for farm children to attend high school they would have had to pay room and board in someone's home and the Derksen family finances did not permit this luxury. Consequently after eight years of school she stayed at home to help her parents with the farm and housework or assist in the homes of her brothers and sisters as she was needed.

The Derksen family loved music. They often had company from other areas and during one such visit Anna and Gerhard expressed a desire for their children to play an instrument. The visitor commented, "How can they learn if you don't have an instrument?" With his encouragement, they invested in an organ. Maria's older sisters took a few lessons but did not show an interest in playing. Maria was fortunate to have a very musically talented teacher, Agnes Neufeld Cornelson in school, who taught her students how to read notes. With just five lessons to her benefit at the age of ten Maria went home and practiced these lessons on the organ. Observing that she had talent her parents encouraged her to play. Eventually she played in churches in each of the places she lived throughout her life. Many people were blessed by her music she shared with others - whether it was at home, church, or a nursing home.

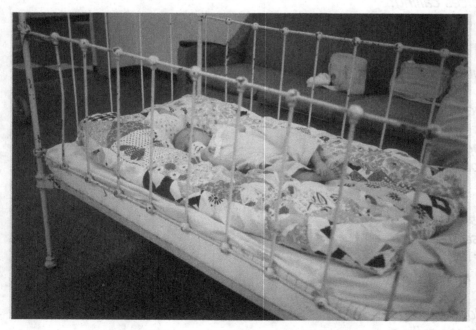

This is the actual crib that George and Anna Derksen used with some of their children. It is a known fact that the two youngest children Susie and Henry both slept in this crib. Note: the style of this crib and compare it to today's requirements.

The King George School 1926

Agnes (Neufeld) Cornelson-Teacher at King George School 1922-1925
First organist

Left: The music teacher who had a profound
Influence on Maria Derksen as a young child.

Agnes Neufeld Cornelson also lived at the
Derksen home during the time she taught at the
King George School.

Grandma and her daughters – August 24, 1924
Back row Left to Right:
Ella, Sarah, Tina, Margaret, Elizabeth, Agnes, Anna, Justina
Front Row: Susie, Grandma (in the chair), Maria

Maria Derksen (1925) is on the extreme right

This picture was taken in 1926.
Back row: Agnes, a friend – name unknown, Tina
Front row: Susie, Ella, Elizabeth and Maria (15).

These pictures were taken in 1926 with her friends
Left Picture: with Susie Mathies
Right picture: with a friend by the name of Hildegard Klassen

Chapter 5

A View of the World in Maria's Youth

Maria would have been 6 or 7 when she attended school for the first time. By the time she was three years old, World War I (1914-1918) had already broken out in Europe. Although Samuel Morse had invented the telegraph in 1835, news would have been slow in coming to Canada from the war front.

In 1917 an important historical event happened. Canadian newspapers banded together to form The Canadian Press. This was a news-gathering co-operative similar to the American UP (United Press) ensuring that the news received at one end of the country would be available to papers at the other end. For the first time through the use of telegraph wires, Canadian readers were in immediate touch with events from anywhere in the world.

This is how they learned of the Battle of Vimy Ridge in 1917. A unified Canadian force of troops under a Canadian command (the 46th South Saskatchewan Battalion known as the Suicide Battalion) recaptured the fortified German Hill 145 that neither the British or French command had been unable to capture. In doing so over 10,000 soldiers were wounded and over 3,500 Canadians lost their lives including one of their own boys, Victor Tallus. He was the 4th casualty to die in this battle. All told 14 Borden area men who had enlisted in WWI gave their lives for freedom. Today there is a memorial set up in the town of Borden honoring the lives lost in this war.

In 1918, when Maria was six years old, World War I, "the war to end all wars", had ended. When the soldiers came home from the front, they brought the Spanish Flu with them. It lingered for approximately 18 months. The total estimated deaths caused by this flu was somewhere between 25 and 50 million people worldwide. Of the Derksen household, Maria and her parents were the only ones who did not get this flu. Other members of her family became very ill but recovered. To combat this virus all schools, theatres, and public buildings were closed in some areas. Maria considered herself to be very blessed with good health. In fact, she didn't even get the measles when exposed to it.

Another event that shaped Maria's time was Prohibition. Prohibition is defined as an act, law or decree forbidding anyone to make or sell alcoholic beverages in a country. Both Canada and the United States went through prohibition though not at the same time. In 1918 Prime Minister Borden signed a law putting into effect a total prohibition across Canada. On January 16, 1920, President Woodrow Wilson of the United States signed into law the 18th amendment also called the Volstead Act. This Act halted the manufacture and selling of any liquor more than .5% alcohol in the United States. This law was in effect until 1933 when it was repealed by the 21st Amendment.

When the manufacturing and sales of liquor was forbidden, people became creative to obtain what was freely available. Many produced their own drink in distilleries drawing women and children to sample the goods. They smuggled the drink across the border in many ingenious ways. These included cutting gas tanks in half filling half the tank with booze and the other half with gas. They created false books and hollow canes. Perhaps the best ploy of all was to wrap their bottles in baby blankets tenderly cradling these "babies".

For every action, there is a reaction, which sometimes has long reaching consequences. Prohibition changed the way people thought. The younger generation desiring to seen as "hip", viewed the bottle as a glamorous adventure. On the flip side, old stock Americans as well as newly arrived immigrants did not like to be told what they could or could not drink, therefore, drinking out of spite and defiance to violate the principle of the 18th Amendment.

The Mennonite Role in Prohibition

We need to examine the role Mennonites had, if any, in the attempt to support laws forbidding the selling and drinking of intoxicating drink. The Temperance movement was not an original idea in the United States. As long as the use of intoxicating or alcoholic drinks has been around, attempts to educate, reduce alcoholic consumption or require abstinence of such drink have also existed. The reasons for moving forward with Prohibition were based on religious as well as political and moral reasons.

The Mennonite Brethren Church founders became staunch supporters of the temperance movement, embracing the concept of absolutely no alcohol. This did not forbid the moderate drinking of wine and beer but prohibited drinks with high alcohol content. This had always been one of their principles. Mennonites also got behind the Anti-Saloon League.

By the early 20th century, most Mennonites had become total abstainers using unfermented grape juice instead of wine for communion. In the 50's the Glenbush M.B. Church was still using wine. Many Mennonites became involved in the politics of the movement supporting the 18th amendment and voted in local option elections where a community was given the right to decide for themselves if they wanted liquor served in their area. More often than not, they voted against it. Because of the breakdown that caused Prohibition to fail, Mennonites withdrew from politics and voting on various issues. It was evident to them that legislation could not enforce these high ethical standards on the population if the majority did not want it or believe in it.

As a side note, in 1972 50% of the Mennonite church members (this included the General Conference Mennonite, Evangelical Mennonite, Mennonite Brethren and Brethren in Christ Church) supported the Mennonite position of total abstinence. In 1989 this percentage dropped to 43%.

Chapter 6

Maria's Salvation Story

Each year the church would devote one or two weeks to holding evangelistic meetings. Bible studies would be held in the mornings with evangelistic meetings held in the evening where visiting speakers would come and speak to the congregation. These speakers more often than not would stay in the Derksen home. This most likely influenced the Derksen children to marry Godly mates.

As one looks through the genealogy of the Derksen the family circle includes a large number of pastors, missionaries, and Christian teachers. Deuteronomy 6 tells us that we are to teach our children and introduce them to the way of God. It states that we are to talk about it wherever we are – sitting at home, or walking in the street. Talk about it from the time we get up in the morning to the time we fall into bed at night. Anna and Gerhard took this responsibility very seriously. In her writings, Anna Derksen states that they prayed often that the Lord would give them grace so that all of their children would be saved as well.

During Maria's 13th year, under the teaching of visiting speaker C.N. Hiebert, she fell under the conviction of the Holy Spirit and realized that she was a sinner and needed a personal Savior. On the suggestion of her sister, Sara, she went to the church for help. On January 15, 1925, she was born again. That night after the evening service she told her parents that she wanted to accept Jesus Christ as her Savior. They prayed with her and explained John 3:16, "God so loved the world that he gave his one and only son, that whoever believes in him shall not perish but have eternal life". At first she could not grasp this truth that God loved the world so much that he sent Jesus to die for her, Maria. She states that she left the room to go outside and looked to the heavens. The stars were shining so bright. It then became very clear to her that the God who made the heavens also welcomed her into his family. When she made that decision, the angels in heaven were rejoicing for a sinner had come home.

Three years later on August 10, 1928 she was baptized and joined the Mennonite Brethren Church. Like her parents before her, she never regretted this decision. One song that strongly reflects Maria's experience is "It Took A Miracle", written by Mr. John W. Peterson and based on Psalms 19. In this Psalms, David talks about the beauty of nature that God had created, but that the greatest miracle of all was the sending of Jesus to earth as a baby to die for our sins.

It Took a Miracle

by John W. Peterson

*1. My Father is omnipotent
And that you can't deny;
A God of might and miracles -
'Tis written in the sky.*

*2. Tho here His glory has been shown,
We still can't fully see
The wonders of His might, His throne-
'Twill take eternity.*

*3. The Bible tells us of His pow'r
And wisdom all way thru,
And ev'ry little bird and flow'r
Are testimonies too.*

*Chorus:
It took a miracle to put the stars in place,
It took a miracle to hang the world in space;
But when He saved my soul, cleansed and made me whole,
It took a miracle of love and grace!*

The Derksen home in 1926

Maria In front of Long Lake where she was baptized
with her second husband, Abe

Chapter 7

Maria Furthers her Education

During the 20's, Maria moved from being a young child in school to lliving life at home with her parents. She completed eighth grade in 1925 and then she stayed at home helping her parents and learning the arts of housekeeping, which would prepare her for life beyond the home.

She attended BBI (Bethany Bible Institute - now Bethany College) in Hepburn, Saskatchewan in 1928 and 1929. At one point, her father did not think that it was necessary for girls to gain further education. It never crossed his mind that girls would want to do this since in that day, girls grew up, got married, and started their own families. Every family has a person who is willing to break the mold of the way things are and do something out of the ordinary for that era. In the Derksen family this person was daughter Agnes. Six years older than Maria, Agnes expressed a desire to go to Bible School and for three years she patiently prayed for this to happen. During the third year of waiting, her father gave his permission for her to attend the Herbert Bible School in Herbert, Sask. that had already been established for a number of years. From that time on, each of the younger Derksen girls had or was given the opportunity to attend Bible school.

Prior to the establishment of the official higher schools of learning, the Mennonite Brethren churches experimented with having traveling Bible classes taught in various churches starting in the Brotherfield area of Waldheim, Sask. By 1926, the Herbert Bible School in Herbert had been established for 15 years in southern Sask. The M. B. church invited George Harms, a Moody graduate from the Rosthern area, to teach three months of evening classes in Hepburn. More than 30 people attended these classes. Spurred on by this kind of interest on the part of the young, three ministers, Jacob Lepp (Dalmeny), H. A. Willems (Brotherfield) and John Harder (pastor of the Borden church) received the support of the area to establish a Bible school in the northern part of Sask.

The old public school building (an L shaped building) was purchased in Hepburn area for two thousand dollars in 1927. Here they held their classes under the leadership of Mr. Dietrich Esau as its first teacher and principal. The total enrollment was seven students for the first year. At the beginning, the school had a curriculum that covered a period of two years. The three-year program was not implemented until 1932 with the current four-year program beginning in 1934. During the time that Maria attended this rather new school, the course of study was to help young people acquire more Bible knowledge and relate it to life. As the third and fourth year studies were added, they offered more advanced studies to those who showed promise towards Christian service in the church or missions. The mission statement of the school was as follows:

"To give our ...youth foundational Bible instruction in the German and English languages... to wrench our youth away from frivolous pursuits and the contemporary "Zeitgeist" (the spirit/whims of the times)... to nurture the German language as a special possession handed down from our fathers... to raise believing youth for the battle of the faith... [and] to take into account the needs of the congregations in the methodical training of Sunday school teachers and sundry (church) workers." [2] - Bruce Guenther: School calendar of 1937

Maria was privileged to attend this school during the two winters of 1928 and 1929. In 1928 , the student enrollment had increased to 21. During the depression there was great interest in attending Bible school with student numbers exceeding one hundred. At the end of the depression this number dropped greatly perhaps due to the fact that WWII broke out and employment opportunities to support the war effort increased dramatically. After the war, the young were choosing to go to secular colleges rather than acquire Bible knowledge. For whatever reasons, student numbers did not exceed one hundred until 1960 when enthusiasm once again was high, attracting new students to this institute.

The majority of the students who attended this school during the first years were young people from Mennonite homes, although it did attract some students from interdenominational churches. This practice continued until the 40's when a more intentional M. B. identity emerged.

The girls lived in one dormitory that was located close to the school while the boys had to walk approximately half a mile from their dormitory to attend classes. Their living quarters did not have indoor bathrooms; students had to bundle up and go outside to an outhouse. At the time of her admittance, the minimum age was 16 although a 14 year old was admitted on occasion.

Although Maria made many friends there, she was also wooed by some of the young men who attended the school. She did not feel right about entering marriage with any of these men and waited until God brought the right person into her life. Little did she know that the man of God's choosing had already been in the country for three years at that time but had not yet met or even seen him.

The Bethany Bible Institute in 1928

Maria as a student at Bethany Bible Institute in 1929

Bethany Bible Institute class of 1930

The Borden M.B. Church choir in 1928
Maria played the organ for the church at that time.

1934 – the last year that Maria played for the church choir
in Borden. Maria is standing to the right of the conductor, A. A. Nickel.

Maria with her brother Henry in 1934

During her years in Borden she taught
the girls Sunday school class.

Chapter 8

Maria's Husband, Peter Wiens

Peter Peter Peter Wiens was born on January 17, 1908 in a Mennonite colony just west of the Ural Mountains. It was a cold winter day when Peter was born to Maria Eck Wiens and Peter Peter Wiens. He was the fifth child and only son born to this union. His grandparents were Peter and Maria Born Wiens. Originally spelled Vien, the name 'Wiens' originates from the word 'Vienna' which in Latin translates to 'a fine tasty wine'.

The colony where Peter was born was Jurmankey, in the province of Ufa (see Map 4). It was located in the Northwest part of the Urals. The capital city of Ufa was also called Ufa, and it was the center of political and social activity. The colony was full of young families just starting out. This was because unless they received financial assistance from their fathers, young farmers could not afford to buy their own land in Southern Russia. However, the price of land in Ufa was cheaper than in Southern Russia therefore it was mainly these young families who decided to move northward and arrived in the Ufa area. Most arrived during the time period of 1894-1901, though some came earlier and others later. The parents of our Peter Wiens were among those early pioneers. These pioneers came from such places as Altsamara, Neu Samara (the birthplace of Maria Eck – Peter's mother) as well as the original mother colony – Molotschna. They came from all walks of life – mill owners, machine manufacturers, merchants, farmers, etc. Ufa was later renamed Baschkir Republic. The largest city in the area near Jurmankey was Dawlekanowa, which was a busy center of activity that included both Mennonite and Russian schools as well as a railroad.

The winters were very severe with storms so blinding one could not see his own hand in front of his face. On the other hand, summers were warm and often dry. Living on a large farm, the Wiens family used horses along with the aid of servants known as Tartars or Russians. The Tartars were Mohammedans (Muslims) whose religion required that they be hospitable. They were deeply religious. Their mosques were called the House of Worship but they habitually prayed in the open wherever they were when their leader known as the Mula sounded the call for prayer at sundown. The Tartars also had a refreshing drink made from the fermented milk of mares called Kumys. It was sometimes said of their Tartars that once given a task to do, they were not known to be reliable in completing it even though they initially agreed to do so.

They helped on the farms with the women acting as nursemaids or 'kindermadchen' and assisted with all of the sewing and cooking which had to be done from scratch. Their payment was in the form of food and gifts.

PETER'S PARENTAGE

Peter's Mother

Maria Eck, was born September 27, 1879 of unknown parentage in Neu Samara and was adopted by Johann and Sara Wedel. Maria's mother died giving birth to her 8th child and Mrs. Wedel was the attending midwife. The Wedels were childless and adopted Maria as their own child since her biological father was unable to support all of his children and made the painful decision to give up the youngest child. Maria grew up loving and respecting this family. The Wedels later adopted another child, a son.

Peter's Father

Few things are known about Peter's father. He was born June 24, 1867 and died on April 28, 1909 at 43 years of age. As a widower, he married Maria Eck Wedel on September 24, 1898 with the birth of their first child Sara occurring in October of that year. Three other daughters followed – Justina (1901), Margareta (1903) and Lena (1905). His daughter Lena died in 1911. The one thing that we do know about Peter's birth father is that he donated the land for the first M.B. church in the area. He died 1909 when Peter was just a year old. In January of 1909, his father was caught in a bad storm and the only way to find his way home was to use the ropes installed by the side of the road, following them to certain points. With one hand holding onto the rope, he used the other to guide the sleigh and somehow got home. Unfortunately he became very ill. This turned into pneumonia, which in turn led to tuberculosis that caused his death a few months later in April of the same year.

Maria Eck's Second Husband, Heinrich Pauls

Maria Wiens married Peter Heinrich Pauls, a bachelor, on January 10 of 1910. This union was blessed with four more children – Katarina (Tina), Hans, Mariachen, and Agnessa (Njessa). Hans and Mariachen died within days of each other in 1917 during a dysentery epidemic.

The Wiens-Pauls family were all musically talented and all members were capable of playing various instruments including violin, mandolin, and guitar. When their neighbors, the Kornelius Siemens (Justina's parents-in-law) came over, they became one big choir.

They were a close-knit family. Everyone in the family was involved in their activities – grandparents, aunts, uncles and kids. The family would clear out the living room and have all the chairs stacked out of the way to play games such as "Blind Man's

Bluff". Other forms of entertainment included reading books and making up their own games.

Almost all of the families in the colony were farmers. Their homes were situated in front by the road with their farms in the back. The children were included in running the farm at a very young age doing chores such as milking cows and gathering eggs. The family raised pigs, cows, chickens and horses. The book UFA has a map (see Map 5) indicating where different people lived. It is presumed that the square marked 'Wedel' is the family that adopted and raised Maria.

As a young boy, Peter was quite strong willed. He did not like to hear the word 'no'. One incident that a relative relayed about him goes like this:

"Peter did not like to hear his mother say that certain two lettered word, NO about something – and proceeded to throw a royal fit. There was a cradle in the room, which was used for the newest baby. This cradle had sharp corners on it. When he couldn't have his own way, he threw himself onto the hardwood floor and bumped his head on a corner of the cradle splitting his head open. His mother fixed him as best as she could and asked him, "Well, Peter do you want to do that again"? One can only imagine what his answer was."

The Wiens-Pauls family did a lot of talking together. The theory that children should be seen and not heard was not adhered to. Children and their feelings were important to their parents; they were encouraged to say what they thought around the table. Their parents were people who loved the Lord greatly and took great pains to invest Christian values in their children, faithfully taking them to church each week. The church was some distance away from the home and in order to keep warm in the winter, straw was thrown on the bottom of the sleigh with blankets covering that. The children were tucked in the sleigh covered by more blankets and kept warm with the use of hot rocks and sad irons. A standard greeting they may have heard their pastor use would probably have gone like this:

"I desire for this assembly the Peace of God which the world can neither give nor take away, which was established on Golgotha and which will not pass away though all else may vanish".[4]

Peter's parents were generous people – sharing what they had with those in need. Some of the people they helped daily were the hungry beggars who came to their door at dusk. They had a room specially set aside to house them overnight. The following morning the straw mattress bags were taken out and clean straw was put in so that no disease or lice would be passed onto the children or the next night's visitors. And every day a large caldron of unpeeled potatoes was washed and cooked and handed to the beggars at the door.

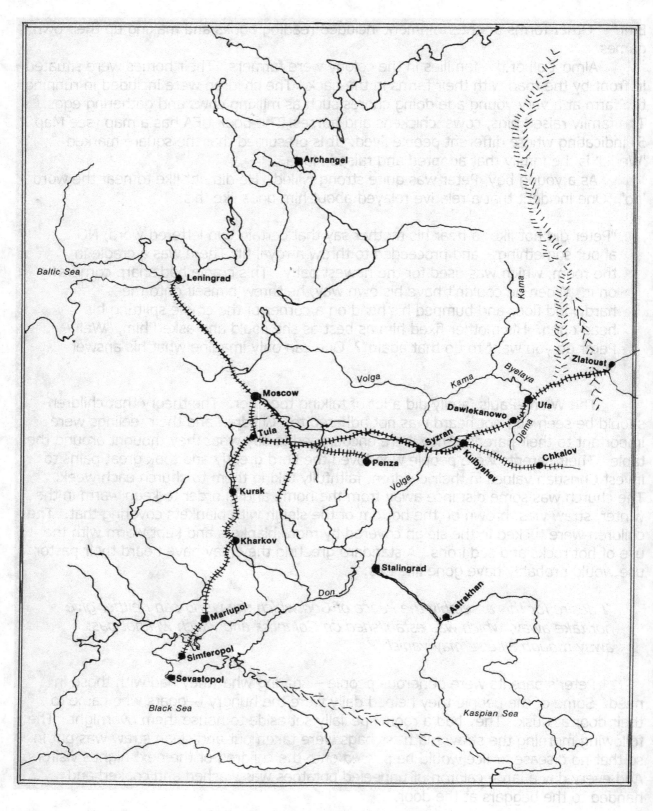

Map 3

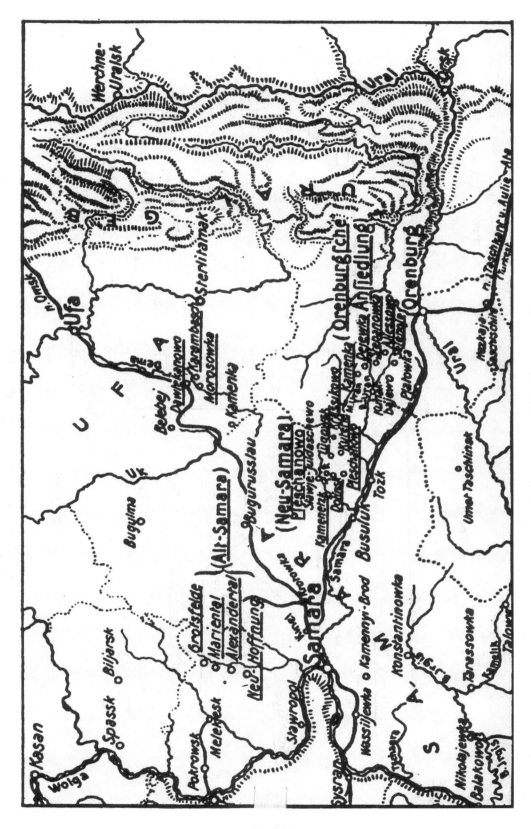

Map 4

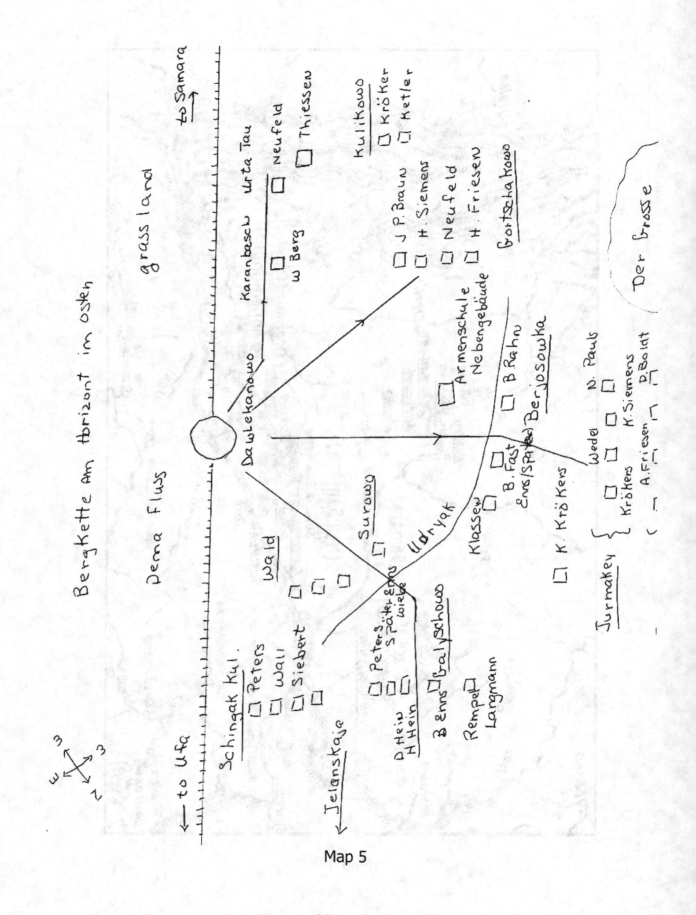

Map 5

Peter's Grandmother
Maria Born Wiens

The Wiens Children
Back row: Justina; middle row: Sara
Front row: Margaret and Peter

The identity of the little girl in front row is unknown

Peter's mother
Maria Eck Wiens

Maria Eck Wiens Pauls suffered much difficulty in her life through the loss of two husbands, several children and the loss of property during the Communistic rule.

She was never the same after the loss of her husband, whose fate she never officially learned. She lived with her two daughters, Tina and Njessa until her death on her birthday on September 27, 1947. She was 68 years old.

Chapter 9

Peter Wiens Escapes to Canada

Russia In Revolution

Before Peter and Maria were eight years old, things were happening which would have a profound impact on their lives. The war to end all wars still had two more years to go. In the midst of all this, a revolution was taking shape.

During the 16th to 18th centuries, Russia was ruled by czars who were very repressive. With the passing of time they gathered massive territories together with great power in Europe. During this time period, Europe was going through unsettling difficulties such as an industrial revolution. Because of its location, Russia was isolated from the western world, which protected them from this unrest. After the defeat of the Russian army in the Crimean War in 1856, the reigning czar of Russia, Alexander II introduced reforms to try to bring Russia into the modern world. One of these reforms was the elimination of serfdom. During the 18th and 19th century, Russia had in their system hierarchy feudal classes. In the feudal system, a person was attached to a Lord and was required to work for him in exchange for certain legal or customary rights. Czar Alexander II abolished this source of labor.

Unfortunately reforms and problems go hand in hand. When all the serfs were freed, it also restricted opportunities for modernizing Russia. As the economy changed, the peasants became more and more discontent. On top of that, Alexander II did not include any kind of representation at the national level where the common person could have a voice. By 1900 many religious and ethnic minorities resided within the borders of Russia. With such a diversity of groups – Mennonites, Tartars etc, there was a movement afoot to "russify" these foreign groups. The government wanted to turn them into good Russians who would support all that the government stood for – military, etc. This they tried to do through the discrimination of policies they implemented and when that didn't do the trick, they started to persecute these non-conformists, which lead to discontentment within their ranks.

When the industrial revolution reached Russia, the working class and development of new industrial centers were affected. It was as if someone took off their blinders exposing to them how poor their living and working conditions were. Consequently, two different problems occurred. Peasants wanted more land, which was becoming scarce and the ranks of the working class were rapidly growing as well. In an effort to bring his subjects under control, the czar Nicholas II took more action to mold the discontented working class and peasants into more obedient moldable citizens. This started a struggle between the peasants and working class.

In 1903 the Second Congress of the Russian Social Democratic Labor Party hereafter referred to as RSDLP convened. The Congress consisted of two parties – one was the Mensheviks (the minority party) and the other the Bolsheviks (the majority). To understand these two parties, one must understand how different they were in their beliefs.

The Mensheviks – the Liberal minority – favored an open party membership and cooperation with other socialist and even some non-socialist groups in Russia.

The Bolsheviks, on the other hand, believed in limiting party membership to fulltime professional revolutionaries who wanted to be part of a tight knit centralized hierarchy with the intent of achieving power. They refused to work with non-extreme parties (democratic parties) such as the Bourgeois. They viewed anyone who owned property, namely the middle class, as capitalists.

The Russian population was made up of two different kinds of people. The Bourgeois society was made up of a small but powerful faction who controlled the factories and owned large estates. They were viewed as being capitalists. The second, but overwhelming population was made up of the proletarians (poor working class) and those who found it necessary to work as their financial economics demanded. This type of system created social inequalities with a wide gulf between the rich and the poor; the haves and the have-nots; the exploiters and the exploited.

Vladimir Lenin, a revolutionary, was able to convince the RSDLP to elect him as leader of the party. His aim was to achieve solidarity between the workers of Russia and Germany and the world. With time, Lenin gained more and more power.

In addition to the peasant-working class struggle for rights, the czar was having governmental troubles of his own. World War I broke out and Russia joined the ranks of the Allies. The industrial revolution was put on hold. Czar Nicholas II ran the military and the war while his wife, Empress Alexandria, took over the administration. With the aid of a fake faith healer, she discredited her husband, shaming him at home. The events of the times revealed that political changes were urgently needed. Unable to hold his government together, the Czarist regime under Nicholas II fell apart forcing the Czar to resign in February 1917. A western style provisional government was set up.

Seeing his opportunity for control, Lenin returned after being in exile, defeated the hostile military and political forces, and overthrew the provisional government, unifying their authority in much of the former Russian Empire.

Lenin's goal was to share the wealth with everyone. No one would be poor – share and share alike. They aimed to replace privately owned property with everyone owning a piece of the pie in matters of production and labor exchange. This would ultimately dissolve the classes and reduce the gap between the bourgeois and the poor. Their goals to protect the working class by (1) limiting their working hours to 8 hours per day; (2) free and compulsory education for children up to 16 years; (3) free medical services for workers at the employers' expense; (4) state pensions for the old and disabled at the capitalists expense; (5) abolish all indirect taxation replacing it with a gradual tax on incomes and inheritances; and (6) returning to the peasants all land and money taken from them by confiscating church property as well as land owned by the tsar, the tsar's immediate family and all governmental agencies.

By October of 1917, with the support of the working class, Lenin executed a bloodless revolution. This became known as the October Revolution. Among his supporters were a large number of Jews. Ironically when Stalin came to power in the 1930's, he purged the Old Guard Jews. After he achieved the success and control that he wanted, Lenin banned the Menshevik as well as all other socialistic organizations from government and set up a "dictatorship of the proletariat" – absolute control over the working class. He dealt harshly with those who did not support him and considered them "enemies of the state", sometimes executing them and sometimes sending any political opponents to forced labor camps which had been previously set up for political dissidents and common criminals. He established the secret police empowering them to arrest or shoot anyone they deemed necessary.

Attaining success and keeping control of what you have accomplished are two different things. The Bolsheviks, convinced that this revolution was going to go worldwide, sped up the construction of the socialistic state in Russia. Marxist believers said that 'capitalism would dig its own grave' because the conflicts that were present in the industrial capitalistic world were about to be reconciled.

Within three years of the onset of the revolution, Lenin had taken over all businesses with more than ten employees. Strikes were banned and labor was mandatory. Money became nonexistent when the state took over production and distribution. The free market was replaced with a state organized barter system. Remember the serfs and serfdom? The government forced the poor peasants to pick sides against the kulaks (wealthy peasants). This resulted in hatred leading to a civil war (1919-1921).

To keep his power and revolution intact, Lenin set up the CHEKA (All- Russian Extraordinary Commission for Fighting Counter-Revolution and Sabotage) to act as the 'revolutionary conscience' with the sacred duty to protect the revolution. The CHEKA, during the course of their responsibility, acted on the concept of killing people not for what they did but rather who they were and what their connections were.

Open civil war broke out between the Red Army (Bolsheviks) and the White Army (Anti-Bolsheviks). The White Army had the support of the Allies who sent over 100,000 troops as well as supplies. To maintain control, Lenin resorted to strengthening his dictatorial powers suppressing all opposition. He moved, as one historian put it, from 'a dictatorship of the proletariat (the poor) to a dictatorship of repression'. The White Army never had the support of the peasants. In areas where they had control, they restored the property of the landlords rather than giving the peasants a piece of the pot. Thus the Reds defeated the White Army.

After the Civil War, Russia had to deal with the problems of famine. Their agriculture output had dropped 30%. Under the Treaty of Brest-Litovsk, Russia lost 1/3 of their population, 80% of its iron and 90% of its coal not to mention the loss of the entire Ukraine, the breadbasket of the Soviet Union, plus other properties they had spent 300 years acquiring. By now even the Russian people despaired of this revolution. They were losing worldwide support and wanted to get on with their lives. Splits were occurring within the Communist party. Lenin was suffering from ill health and was becoming weaker and weaker. On the other hand, Stalin, the Secretary of the Communist Party, was becoming stronger and stronger. Stalin's power came from here and from there.

After the death of Lenin in 1924, Stalin, with the help of three other men, took over the control of the Bolsheviks. One of the mistakes the Bolsheviks made was trying to make the industrial revolution move faster than it should. Stalin believed that goals were reached gradually over time. Once Stalin got what he wanted, he disposed of any opposition that stood in his way. In 1922, he pulled all the little countries within the Soviet boundaries together, renaming them The Union of the Socialist Soviet Republics (USSR). The running of this Republic was done from Moscow. Everything – war, foreign policy, trade, and finance – would be controlled there. From there Stalin controlled all party appointments, promotions and demotions. By 1927, Stalin had already sent into exile the men who had helped him succeed and was ready to put into place the Stalin Revolution. Stalin was also responsible for the execution of the exiled czar Nicholas II and his entire family on July 18, 1918.

It was during this time period, (1921-1929) that approximately 29,000 Mennonites immigrated to other countries, with a large percentage coming to Canada. Famine, civil war and persecution forced them to make a change. In 1930 Stalin closed the borders to further emigration.

Effects of the Soviet Political Unrest On The Mennonites

Outside influences, particularly political and general religious atmospheres, forced the family to make painful decisions in the following years. Even before Bolshevism took over in 1917, Russia had already experienced many years of political unrest.

On November 3, 1914 a decree was published that prohibited the use of speaking in German, their mother tongue, in both the public assemblies and the press. In 1915 they also passed strict liquidation laws in which some people found themselves without land overnight. During the years of political instability and civil wars, the parents were forced to house many soldiers overnight. The church in general – Lutheran, Baptist or Mennonite – played an important position in Soviet life. A great deal of constitutional legislation establishing the church on a strict ecclesiastical basis was passed in 1917 by the church council but most of it could not be put into action under the new Soviet regime.

While the M.B church was separated from the state under the provisional government, it was also persecuted. In the eyes of the law, the church had to be deprived of any and all means of being influential over national life with the intent of rebuilding national life on antireligious patterns. The Russian Revolution, a.k.a. Bolshevism, dramatically altered the role the church played in community life. By 1917, Russia was facing major problems. Cold, hungry, demoralized by the war, the people were looking for a Savior. With the impending collapse of his country, under the severe pressure of revolutionary groups, Tsar Nicholas II abdicated his throne on March 2, 1917. When his brother, Michael, refused the crown, a provisional government was set up.

At this point, Lenin was determined to overthrow the government – a goal he achieved by October 25, 1917. Having embraced Marxist principles in 1889, he believed he could lead a backward Russia into a modern world. The goals of the Bolshevik Revolution were threefold:

1. Create a paradise or utopia on earth where there was no injustice.
2. Each worker would be a master in his own factory.
3. Private property would be forbidden, thus paving the way for each citizen to share the wealth equally.

Churches were now prohibited from any educational activities i.e. private schools, seminaries etc. or any missionary expansion. In order to enforce this edict, the government destroyed churches and imposed heavy taxes on them. They deported and executed both clergy and active laymen alike as they saw fit to change a strong vibrant church community into an irreligious body disrupting church administration.

Attempts were made to establish government-sponsored churches competing with the historical church, but these attempts did not attract many believers. The government sponsored churches operating under names such as the Living Church, and the Renovated Church did not survive very long. One of the former bishops, Sergius of Gorki, was permitted to assume the leadership of the church but the government controlled his movements.

Without a doubt, the Mennonite church known for its passive nature with regards to any military activity were not willing to bend under the governmental pressures and therefore had to be equally willing to suffer the consequences. They would not comply with the government-sponsored church. It is under these conditions that the next chapter of the Wiens children unfolded.

Founding of the Mennonite Central Committee (MCC)

The aftermath of the revolution and war left Russia facing a terrible famine from 1921 to 1923 in which thousands of people died. As a result of the revolution, war, famine, and typhus some 2,200 Mennonites died in Russia as these problems spread throughout the land. Peter's third oldest sister, Margareta, was one of the victims of typhus losing all of her hair in the course of the disease.

In an effort to ease some of these problems, the Mennonites sent four men to North America to search for possibilities of land and to plead their case with the Mennonite church in Canada to help their hungry Russian brothers and sisters. The Mennonite Central Committee (MCC) was formed on September 27, 1920 to assist these four men in any way they could. MCC was founded as a co-operation of 15 different Mennonite church groups and the Brethren of Christ. Sharing a common goal of serving the sick, hungry, and thirsty, they formed themselves into one central committee from which all other relief efforts flowed. In the 16th century, Menno Simons made this statement that has become the driving force behind their mission.

"True evangelical faith cannot lie sleeping, it clothes the naked, it comforts the sorrowful, it feeds the hungry, it shelters the destitute, it cares for the sick, and it becomes all things to all men."[6]

They were motivated by the fact that they had seen and/or experienced hunger, war, and the refugee plight in the Soviet Union and Europe.

It was these desperate and difficult economic, political, and religious pressures that set the stage for the future of the Wiens family.

Canada Bound

By 1925 things were very difficult politically. In 1918 Sara married a clergyman, Nicolai Pauls. One Sunday morning in February, Nicolai preached in the morning. Later, during their noon meal, the police broke into their home on the pretense of looking for guns. Finding no guns, with pistols facing him from either side, they forced Nicolai out into the yard to shoot him. God was at work and protected this young minister by jamming the guns. They tried to shoot Nicolai again, and again God intervened on the Pauls' behalf. The police, now very angry and frustrated, got back onto their horses and rode away. Nicolai went back into his home and told Sara that for their safety, it was time to move to Canada.

Peter and his sister, Margareta (who was still single but engaged to John Enns at this time) also wanted to go to Canada, but their parents did not want to let them go because they were both so young. Peter was now 16 and approaching the military draft age. In 1880, the Russian government had abolished all special privileges from non-Russian settlers in South Russia, including the exemption from military service. Therefore he wanted to leave while he still had the opportunity to do so and escape the unsettling military conditions. To ease their parents' minds, Nick and Sara offered to sponsor Peter and Margareta and help them along as much as possible. The group of eight included Peter and Margareta, Nick and Sara, and their four children (Heinrich, Maria, Peter and Nicolai - aged one thru six). They arrived on the shores of Quebec on June 6, 1925

Their mother Maria wanted to emigrate with them as well but her husband was not ready to make such a big decision, although he did help them financially. The parting of the Canada bound children from all family ties in Russia was sad, but after much prayer their parents let them go. They understood Nick and Sara had to leave because of the threats to Nick's life. From the incident at the noon meal until their departure, Nick was a marked man and could be taken away at any time. This group was among the first of the Mennonites to leave.

Between the years of 1922 to 1930, 25,000 Mennonites left Russia to escape the grip of spreading communism. Most of them (21,000) settled in Canada while the rest went to Paraguay, Brazil and Mexico. The last wave of immigrants did not leave until the years of 1941 through 1943. This wave consisted of 35,000 participants, but only 12,000 successfully managed to reach other nations.

Whether they left or stayed was really a matter of conscience, and there were many individual reasons. Some of those who stayed were too comfortable in their ways and didn't see any real threat invading their lives. Others felt that God had called the Mennonites to Russia for a purpose, and therefore it was the will of God to stay. Many who did leave felt that more than the loss of their military service exemption, which was honored until the late 1920's, was at stake. They would also lose their right to operate any undisturbed church activities, which included their own institutions caring for the sick, the disabled, and the old. They wanted the right to teach their children Christian values as they saw fit, which was very important for the survival of the Mennonite church.

Every effort was made on the part of Nick and Sara to bring the family over but to no avail. Perhaps the biggest reason Peter's stepfather, Mr. Pauls, could not make the decision to leave was because he felt that things were not as bad as they seemed. One story that was told was that Mr. Pauls had been persuaded by one of his brothers to stay and was convinced that maybe he would still have time to leave later on. Perhaps his brother too, felt that there was no real threat facing them in staying.

However, things got progressively worse after 1925. Daughter Justina left with her husband, Kornelius K. Siemens, and their two children, Kornelius and Nellie in 1926. By the early 30's, the borders were closed and no one else was allowed out. Very few were allowed to leave in the 40's. When Peter's half sister, Njessa, was ten years old the remaining family left behind in Russia was forced to leave their home and all of their possessions to go to a resettlement camp in Siberia. Their stepfather, Peter Pauls, had been sent away once in 1929. In the summer of 1931 they were again relocated. Thus, this was the plight facing Mennonite families left behind for one reason or another.

Unfortunately, Mr. Pauls was taken away twice and disappeared for the final time in 1937. Before his final disappearance, men were already being taken from their villages and sent to the central part of Siberia to settle in the forests there. One day all the men from the village where the Pauls family lived failed to come home. Political security was so tight that when the women inquired about their husbands, they were simply told that if they asked for their husbands again they would be taken to the same place. The police left only the women and children behind to fend for themselves. Maria Pauls was never the same after this and her daughters, Tina and Njessa, took care of her from that time on until her death on her 68th Birthday-Sept.27, 1947.

There are several theories about what may have happened to the men. They may have been sent into Siberia. They may have been locked in a boxcar, which had gas poured over it and lit, burning the men alive. This was common in some cases. Another story we have heard is that the men were taken out and shot. Yet another possibility was that he was thrown into prison and later died around 1943. At any rate, they never saw their families again. Because of all the possibilities of what may have happened, the exact date of Peter Pauls' death is not known.

Some felt that with their husbands forcibly removed from the scene by the communists, a weak link was created in the homes of these women since every able-bodied person was required to work. Consequently the women were stretched beyond their limits and 'permanently exhausted' trying to tend not only the home and children but also doing the jobs usually given to men such as pulling long hours in a factory or building railroads. Some felt this was part of the Communists plan to eliminate the influences of Christianity in the young. Mothers would have their hands more than full, causing the religious instruction of their children to suffer the most. The Communists were planning to undermine the values of the family's Christian principles, weakening the impact of the church and thus paving the way for the next generation of young people to reject Christianity by filling that void with something more appealing. This generation would then become the founding foundation of an antireligious society, which was important to the success of the establishing and survival of communism.

However, the Mennonite belief was that man's plan could not succeed as they forgot to reckon with the fact that God's power superceded the government's. The Bible tells us "The Lord foils the plans of nations and places hindrances and frustrations in the purposes of mankind" (Psalms 33). Many years later, visitors from Russia to Canada related to their hosts how fortunate they were they could pray together around the table. The Russian believers did not allow their children's religions instruction to suffer, even it meant praying with their children behind a large woolen blanket in a corner, whispering their prayers. Russian believers were willing to pay the ultimate price for the privileges of open prayer, Bible reading and attending church. They paid with the loss of lives and property.

Peter Heinrich Pauls

Peter's Stepfather

Peter Pauls disappeared for the last time in November, 1937

The Wiens Pauls Family 1925
Back row: Margaret, Justina Wiens Siemens, Tina, Peter and Sara Wiens Pauls
Seated: Kornelius Siemens, Maria Eck Wiens Pauls, Njessa, Peter H. Pauls and Nicolai Pauls

Peter with his brothers-in-law
Approximately 1926-27 in Canada

Back row: John Enns, Nick Pauls, Kornelius Siemens
Front Row: Peter Wiens

Peter and his sister, Margareta

This picture was taken in 1925 in Russia
when Peter was 16 and Margareta was 22.
At the time of their departure from Russia,
Margareta was engaged to a fellow
Mennonite believer, Johann Enns. They were
married on November 22, 1925 in Canada.

Njessa (Pauls) Schmidt
With her daughter, Anna on the property
where Peter Wiens grew up.

Below: John Wiens on the same property June 1995

Chapter 10

Peter's Early Life in Canada

New Life In **Saskatchewan** *Canada*

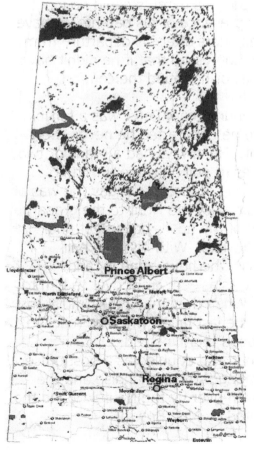

After the travelers arrived in Quebec they traveled by train to Saskatchewan and Peter got a summer job in Balgonie as a farmhand. Balgonie (see inset on next page) is close to Regina. In the fall of 1925 he went to Rosthern Academy where he enjoyed school and did quite well learning English. He returned to work in Balgonie the following summer. He also worked in a lumber camp before joining the Pauls in Glenbush in 1927. In the beginning, times were hard and starting all over again was difficult. The Pauls were among the five families who moved to Glenbush (see inset) from Waldheim in 1927. In 1928, 20 more adults joined their company.

At this time Nick, Sara, and their children were living in a tall granary across the road from where their son, Peter Pauls would later move. The Pauls family suffered great personal loss in their first six months in Canada with the deaths of two of their children (Heinrich and Nicolai). However, they were overjoyed when their daughter, Tina, joined their family.

One of the more humorous episodes of Peter's early life happened in 1927. Now 18 years old, he had heard that there were lots of jack rabbits in Glenbush and sunk his

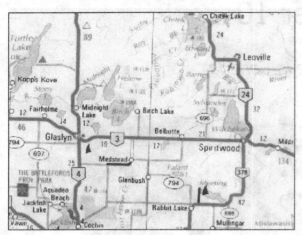

summer savings into some equipment that he thought would make him rich quick. This equipment consisted of a gun and an apparatus with a light similar to that of a coal miner's light. With this light strapped to his head, all he had to do was pull the trigger to shoot the rabbit and the light would go on. With the Pauls' living space still very tight, Sara asked Peter how he was going to dry the skins. "Oh" he replied, "No problem! The top of the granary is tall and I'll just dry them there". He made his home with the Pauls family up until a year before he got married in 1934.

The Wiens children never regretted their decision to leave Russia but undoubtedly experienced homesickness for their family members left behind. Postage for overseas mail was two cents and even that was hard to come up with at times. Nonetheless, they were faithful in keeping correspondence with their parents in Russia. Peter often found it hard to understand why the circumstances in Russia were so difficult and was lonely living among strangers in Canada. His parents could no longer get out as the borders were closed. He longed for the presence of his parents, to have the chance to see them again and to talk to them. Ten years after his departure from Russia, he still found it difficult. In a letter to Maria he confessed that if he didn't have his Savior he would have despaired long ago. In his Savior he found the comfort, wisdom and strength to go on.

As a young man, Peter was a terrible tease. Once he got started he never knew when to quit. He always had a prank or two up his sleeves to pull on some unwitting person. On one particular Sunday, he was at a neighbor's home. He went to the granary where some of the host's boys slept and relaxed for a while. With his eyes half closed, he saw the boys come in, and thinking he was asleep, crept over to him to tie him up. When they made their move to act, he had the last laugh when he reached up and grabbed them instead.

During the 30's Glenbush had a general store that also doubled as a post office. The Harrisons owned the store with one of them operating the merchandise and the other handling the post office. Later this store was taken over by the Neufeld's and the post office had its own little building, which was operated by Mrs. Brown.

Peter bought a farm located five miles east of John and Margaret Enns' in section S.W.-24-49-14-W3rd. One of the things he inherited from his parents was his ability to be willing to share of himself with those around him. During one of the drought years, he provided shelter during the winter months to the Henry Krahns until they moved to their own place. His first independent address was:

Box 2
Glenbush, Sk.

He lived at the farm by himself for about a year before he married Maria Georgina Derksen from Borden, Sask. on October 7, 1934. Together they formed a new home and family.

A Saskatchewan Flag
The background is the Union Jack with the center symbols
Representing Saskatchewan itself

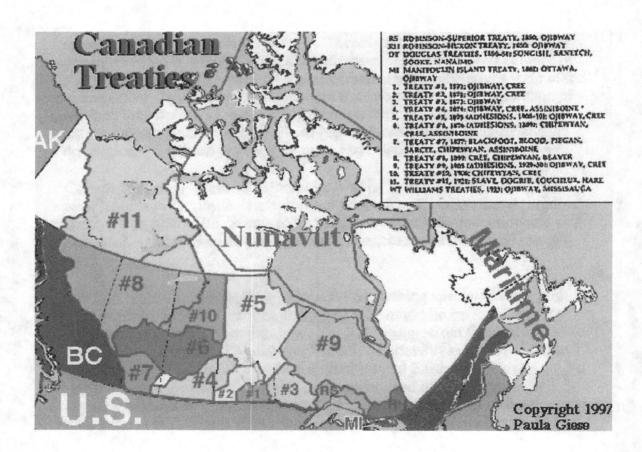

Chapter 11

The Establishment of the Glenbush M. B. Church

One of the priorities that the new pioneers in the Glenbush area had was to meet with each other. In the beginning, the families of both the Mennonite Brethren and the Mennonite General Conference backgrounds had joint services in the Avery School. Some of the M.B. families lived on farms on the other side of town, which was a considerable distance (approximately 10 miles) from the Avery School. The chief form of travel at this time was horse and wagon, so one can only imagine how long it took the various families who lived a distance away to get there.

Considering this factor, the M.B. families moved into the vacant United Church building in town, using it free of charge. Their first service here was in 1928. At first they met every other week and then every week, choosing Nicolai Pauls as their first pastor. The services were held entirely in the German language.

Eventually, they decided to build their own church and bought a parcel of land from the railroad. After an 8' x 10' basement was dug, they constructed a 22' x 32' church. All the lumber for this building was cut on Peter Wiens' sawing outfit. To keep warm, they had a large airtight heater in the middle of the room. The building was completed in 1930 for a total cost of $236.00, and the first service was held in this building in March of 1931.

It is not known when Peter became a Christian but it is believed that he accepted Jesus as his Savior after he arrived in Canada. On September 23 of 1928, the church had their first baptism at Long Lake. Some of the participants baptized and received into the church membership were 20-year-old Peter, his sister Margareta (Greda), her husband John Enns, and Peter Bartels.

The immigrants also brought their musical talents along with them. Peter was in the first male quartet along with Nick Pauls, Henry Zimmerman, and Jake Klassen. The church had a choir led by Nicolai Pauls. Peter sang solos as well as sang in a duet with one of his nephews, Peter Pauls. Together they harmonized so well that people remembered their music many years later.

Do you recall the expression "as poor as church mice"? The Glenbush church did have its share of mice. Rosella Martens, Jake & Mary Klassen's daughter, recalled an incident regarding the church mice.

"I so vividly remember the old church and the occasional mice which would come to the evening service. At one of these services the little mouse sat on your dad's (Peter Wiens) shoe for a while during the singing. He seemed totally unaware – after all he was doing one of the things he did best – singing!"[8]

Peter maintained a high standard of Christian living, which did not allow for any form of compromise. He gained the respect of those around him. He strived to uphold righteousness over flattery or falsehood. Although he was strict, he also saw his imperfections and viewed himself as a 'diamond in the rough'. He resolved in his heart early to be strict, determined, and as hard as steel and brass. He strived to rise against all immorality, unrighteousness, injustice, and flattery. His motto was 'do unto others as you would have them do unto you'. He also desired to be forgiving and to constantly be learning from others, but to let God bring about the results that He desired.

Attending church was very important to Peter. By the time he married Maria Derksen, the church had been established for six years. The Wiens family was very involved in church activities. Peter taught Sunday school and conducted the children's choir while Maria played the piano for the choir and taught Sunday school. Together with some of the older children, he sang tenor in the church choir. On occasion he even conducted an orchestra. When family grew bigger in the 1950's and his two-door Ford was aging, he made two trips to church making sure that each member of his family would be present in the House of the Lord.

In 1952 the church celebrated its 25th anniversary. At that time the pastor, Nicolai Pauls, gave a report about the growth and trials that the families of the church grew through. Below are quotes from that report, used with permission from the Pauls family.

"In reflection on the wonderful direction and gracious help of the Lord in the past 25 years, I want to base my comments on Genesis 32:10 where it says, 'I am unworthy of all the kindness and faithfulness you have shown your servant. I had only my staff when I crossed this Jordan, but now I have become two groups.' These are the words of Jacob's prayer just before he met his brother Esau. The same God, the God of Jacob, was and is our God too. Were we to place the beginning experiences of each one who settled here in the past 25 years in the same context, we too would have to say, I had only my staff."

"In about May of 1927 the Lord sent two families to the MB congregation in Glenbush. H. Kroeker with three small children, one dependent child with his senior mother and his widowed sister, Mrs. Hein, and us with three children. So we began with six members and seven children."

"In July of the same year, three additional couples, A. Dick, and the Newfield's arrived. Brother J. Klassen with daughter Tina and son Jacob came here for the summer months to clear and break land. Here, under the poor and difficult circumstances of the wild bush and stony land we strove to build homes for our families. Here and there, scattered in the bush sat a family or a bachelor, apparently contended and satisfied. Broken acreage was limited and not readily found. The distance between members from Northeast to Southwest was ten miles, but the love for each other overcame all the discomfort of the traveling challenges. The box-wagon offered more room and time for mutual conversation than today's comfortable cars. In spite of the difficult financial situation, we looked to the Mennonite principle to get rich and, according to Scripture, to subdue the earth and flung ourselves into the work."

"The Krokers and us (Nick & Sara Pauls) were given the opportunity to rent some land. Even though it was late, we planted a small crop. In doing so we quickly learned that we were "stone-rich". But the pressing "must" kept us going. The hopefulness of a promising crop encouraged us greatly during that difficult beginning. Brother H. Kroeker often sang the song, "Let The Hearts Be Ever Joyful" (Last Die Herzen Immer Froehlich) during the morning worship hour. However, on the morning of August the 8th of 1927, everything was white. Naturally everything was ruined - the crop was frozen. That morning, "Let The Hearts Be Ever Joyful" was not sung. So now what could we do? We had only one option to sustain our winter existence ... leave home to "workout". We drove to Brotherfield to work on a threshing crew. But here too we were tested. In five weeks we could work only one and a half days ... it was always wet. From time to time we got jobs digging potatoes, digging cisterns, and so on. We were also able to gather plenty of vegetables to take home with us. The Lord helped us and we always had bread, clothes, and shelter."

"In 1928 our group grew by five or six families. Much could be said about the initial experiences of these "brothers and sisters." (J. Klassen, J. Arendt, Bartel, Enns). With constant focus upon the Lord, great effort, enthusiasm and persistence their difficulties were overcome. So it is that over the years our group grew to a settlement of forty families. The fall of 1933 brought a special event. Nearly twenty families from the dry region of the South came to Glenbush. The words of Luke 2:7, "there was no room for them in the inn", found fulfillment. Every place, be it chicken barn or granary served as a home that winter. However, we were thankful for the growth it brought to our church. After a few years we encountered another change. Many members left us, mainly for BC and occasionally other provinces. After that there was a quiet time. From time to time individuals moved away. It was twenty-five years where we interchangeably dwelt on Tabor's Heights and walked through valleys of testing. Yet, today we say, "The Lord has done great things for us; whereof we are glad" (Ps 126:3) To Him be glory and praise for it all."

"Psalms 100:2 says 'Worship the LORD with gladness; come before him with joyful songs.' This was also our desire. The first while, 1927-1928, in early fall we gathered in the Every School with believers from the Mennonite Conference. I am happy to be able to report that it was a good time. The group, of course, was small but love toward one another was big and there was sweet harmony between everyone. I often recall the Christmas Eve with the children and the first New Years Eve in the school. In the summer, or perhaps the early fall of

1928, our MB congregation was given the opportunity to use an English church in town for a while. During that time, the church was in a more central location. A choir was begun, youth meetings were started, regular Sunday services were conducted, and so on. We also had occasional visitors to our church. The Lord's presence and blessing were with us. However, there was a growing desire to acquire our own church in order to conduct services without disturbance or dependence upon others. We began to think, plan, and look around for a suitable location. A $1.50 levy was gathered from each member to build a fund to purchase some church land. This land was found; indeed it was the Northeast corner of this quarter. Because the railroad was close by and the potential for disturbance was significant, it was later decided to locate more to West Side of the same quarter where we now are. We bought this three acres block of land for the reasonable price of $20.00 per acre."

Building of the church

"It was not easy for our small group of resourceless beginners to entertain the thought of building. To begin with we decided to build with logs, so we had to haul these logs from the bush in the north. To cover the minimal cost related to this, we assessed ourselves with a fifty cents fee per member. In August of 1930 we established a fund based on an assessment of $3.00 per member in order to take further steps to build the church. Since the sum of $3.00 fell far short of the needed funds, I (Nicolai Pauls) was given the responsibility of requesting help from other churches. At a district meeting we were allowed to present this request to the churches of the Northern District. Subsequently, I wrote to all seventeen churches in existence at that time and the net result was that our fund grew only by $3.50. We found ourselves exploring further ways and means open to us. In the same year, 1930, because of the difficult financial situation and the shortage of time, the decision was made to build with cheap boards ($15.00 - $18.00). The wood for the frame was cut on two sides from round wood to serve as 2 X 4s. The boards for the inner walls were planed by hand where necessary and the edges of the boards were trimmed with a circular saw.

In October of 1930 we began to build the church. A small basement was dug, the cornerstone (not cement) was laid and the walls were set up. It wasn't always easy to accurately use the square on the round wood but we comforted ourselves with the saying, 'Who drives by quickly does not see the mistakes, and who drives by slowly assumes it should be built that way'. All the grown men participated in the work and I believe it went ahead cooperatively and well. Thanks to the Lord's presence and the great effort and hard work of our brothers and sisters we were able to complete the 24 x 32 foot church building without any accidents during the winter months before March 1931. On March 15, 1931 we were able to conduct our first meeting in our own very simple but debt-free church building. Who could have guessed the bare dollar cost at that time? ($256.00) The next day, immediately after the first meeting, there was a funeral for a small child. So it was that our first celebration was a funeral. On June 21, 1931 we had the privilege of dedicating our miniature meetinghouse to the Lord.

In September 1933 a sixteen-foot addition was put on the West End of the church. This was when the members from the South joined us. In October 1939 the East end was lengthened by sixteen feet and so our tiny house grew till it was 24 by 64 feet large. (Not only in BC do people build big.) What was more, in October 1940 the basement was put under the building. In February of 1943 the inside was completed. We [Sara & Nicolai Pauls] had our Silver wedding there. In June 1948 the church building received an outside "dress". In 1949 the electric light found its place. If we can claim this finished the church, then we can say it took 19 years. If the saying," What takes long, becomes good" is true, then we have a good church building ... something for which we are very thankful today ... and it is debt free."

"Now I come to the spiritual blessings. The Scripture, 'where two or three are gathered in my name' has truly been our experience. Even if it was not literally so, it applied to us in our small numbers. I clearly recall how we met in three different locations because of the distance between us and once a month had a main/central meeting in this venue. The church was established on July 15, 1928 with a founding membership of 18 souls. During these twenty-five years (spoken in 1958) we have had:

23 baptisms in which 178 people were baptized.
We now have 161 members.
6 founding members are here today
40 members were accepted with a certificate of transfer.
115 were baptized here.
The oldest member is 89 years old, the youngest is 11.
7 members were excommunicated.
3 founding members have died.
15 founding members are alive, 6 of who still live in Glenbush.
   *Of the very first people who initially moved here around 1927, only six
   people are left-Us (Sara and Nicolai Pauls) with our three children and the
   Peter Wiens.*
Ordinations
Preachers were ordained here and 2 elsewhere
2 deacons were ordained (1 here, 1 elsewhere)
Weddings
Weddings were conducted here (19 by Nicolai Pauls)
13 Silver weddings (all were young people)
2 Golden weddings
*Deaths ... here I feel like what we read in Psalm 71:7 "I am a wonder unto
many"*
Souls (members and mothers)
10 souls (member's children)
10 souls (of non-members)
*Approximately 39 families with an aggregate count of 251 souls are currently
living here (as of 1958).*
Newly built farms number about 26 in a 10 by 7 mile area."

*"The church that was constructed in 1931 was deemed to be structurally unsafe
and plans were made to build a new church right in town. This building was
not built until around 1963 and is still in use at the time of this writing in 2005.
Both Rose and Lily were married in this building. "*

The First Glenbush M. B.
Church building

Inside the original Church –
note the heater in the aisle
used to keep them warm. The
pews look to be pretty
uncomfortable. No sleeping
here!

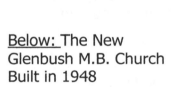

Below: The New
Glenbush M.B. Church
Built in 1948

The Glenbush Mennonite Brethren Church adults
I believe that Peter and Maria are the 4th couple from the right.

The Glenbush church choir in 1946.
Maria is young lady in the center of the front row wearing the hat.

This blanket covering was given to Nick and Sara Pauls on their 25th Wedding Anniversary by the Glenbush church in 1943.

Each lady embroidered a square with a verse of her choice.
The square Maria made is in the second row, second square from the right.

Chapter 12

Courtship and Marriage

Peter first set eyes on Maria when he attended a music course in Laird, Saskatchewan. The main purpose of this event was to learn how to conduct and lead a choir. After each choir sang, the conductors were given an evaluation based on their performance. One of the choirs that gave a performance was the Borden M.B. church whose pianist was a talented and single lady named Maria Derksen. I will let her tell her story of this experience as she relates it.

"In 1933 in July our choir went to Laird to attend a music course for five days. Every choir had to sing and then criticism was given. We also had to conduct. As a group it was fun but standing in front of 100-150 young people alone and conducting them, knowing that you'd be criticized was something else.
There was one young man who was very nervous. He picked up a conducting stick and started conducting but his hand was shaking so hard that he dropped the stick. Everybody laughed very hard because it really was very funny. But the young man stood his ground, picked up a heavier stick, made a joke about it all and started over again. All this made everybody relax and the singing was very lively." [7]

From her piano bench, Maria merely nodded at him and encouraged him to go on. Three months later she received a letter from a young man who had described himself as the conductor who dropped the baton in Laird. He wanted to know if he could come and see her. Maria did not feel the time was right. From the tone of the letters that were found in Maria's possessions, Peter was lonely away so far away from his parents even though he had two married sisters in the area. He did not push their relationship but chose to become better acquainted with her through letters while she waited for an answer from God. He found in her a person he could bare his soul to, expressing his loneliness and desire for a family of his own. Peter was known to be forgetful at times. On one occasion he had not received a letter from Maria for quite a time, only to remember six days later that he had stored the letter he had received from her in a pair of rubber boots which happened to be at someone else's house.

Although he first officially made contact with Maria via correspondence desiring to meet the young lady who had so encouraged him, the timing was wrong. They crossed paths again in the spring of 1934 when he really met her for the very first time.

Maria Georginia Derksen

The young lady who gave him
encouragement in Laird at the music
festival.

The handwriting of Peter Wiens on an envelope dated August 1934

The 1930's were challenging years for Maria Derksen's family. They were years of drought, sorrow, courting, and marriage. In April of 1930, Maria's older sister, Sara Wiebe, died at the age of 31. Her father, Gerhard Derksen, became very ill and entered eternity on August 14 of 1933 at 67 years old. After Maria finished Bible school in 1930, she went back home to help her parents. The Derksen family had saved enough money during the good years so their daughters did not need to find employment in other locations. Maria was involved in church work both as a Sunday school teacher and the choir pianist. By this time the Derksen household consisted of the parents, sister Tina who married in January of 1930, Ella who married in June of 1930, 29 year old Elizabeth, 19 year old Maria, 16 year old Henry, and 15 year old Susie. By the time Maria was married in 1934 the Derksen's were grandparents to 32 grandchildren.

Each year, Maria's parents would take a trip to the Glenbush area to visit friends and relatives. They would always take one child or another but never Maria. When Maria asked her father why they had always taken her older sister Elizabeth but never her, Mr. Derksen replied that he didn't want to take her because there were too many bachelors and he didn't want to lose her to someone there. In 1934 her brother, Henry, took his mother on their annual trip to visit friends and relatives in the Glenbush area and this time took Maria along for the ride. Maria had long indicated an interest in seeing what this part of the country looked like. Her first impression of the area was that of beauty with many trees and lots of uncultivated land. But this trip changed the course of her life, as it was the first time she really met the young bachelor named Peter Wiens. Just as she took the courtship of the young men from her Bible school days to prayer, she took the prospect of marriage with this man to prayer as well, waiting for God to reveal to her which direction to take.

With the exception of her sister Sara, all of her sisters met and married young men from the Borden area. Her courtship with Peter Wiens was different from her sisters'. There was a 90-mile difference in distance between Borden and Glenbush. Their courtship was entirely by mail (postage was two cents at that time) with the exception of three times when he came to see her prior to their marriage. As was the custom in the Derksen home, she was properly chaperoned during this time by another adult.

They were married on Sunday afternoon on October 7, 1934. Following the wedding they had a big supper which Maria's sister, Elizabeth, prepared. Ironically, this wedding was extra special for Elizabeth because it was there that she met her future husband, Isaac Willems, who had been eyeing her for some time. With the Depression in full swing, money was tight and therefore the Wiens had no honeymoon.

Peter & Maria's engagement picture in Borden, 1934.

He did not give her an Engagement ring such as the ones people give today. The diamond engagement ring, as we know it, did not become popular until 1941 or so. The first recorded diamond engagement ring was given to Mary of Burgandy by the Archduke Maximillian of Hamburg in 1477

Peter and Maria's Wedding picture

They were married on October 7, 1934.

She was almost 23 years old.
Peter was 26 years old.

Chapter 13

"Eat It Up, Wear It Out, Make It Do, Or Do Without"
Maria and Peter as Newlyweds in the Era of the Great Depression

On the Tuesday after their wedding, the newlyweds packed up Maria's things into a rented car and traveled to Peter's farm four miles from Glenbush. What now takes no more than 2 hours took them an entire day and they arrived in the dark even though the speed limit was 15 mph. They had three flat tires that Peter needed to fix himself. I will let her describe her new living conditions and her first year in Glenbush:

"The house we lived in was made of logs, far from finished but very warm. The range heated the kitchen and pantry. The space heater kept the living room and bedroom warm. We plastered the walls ourselves and then whitewashed the walls, which were quite nice and clean. The first ten years were tough years because of drought, frost, etc. We didn't have the dust storms that they had in the south because we had too much bush land.

I learned, too, what pioneering work was like. The first winter at Glenbush I was alone at home most of the time. Peter hauled wood from the forest about twelve miles away. He got up at 3:00 a.m., had a hot breakfast, hooked up four strong horses, took lunch along, and drove to the forest. He wanted to drive an empty sleigh in the dark rather than a full load. We had an hour less daylight at Glenbush than we have here (Saskatoon) in winter. By 3:00 pm, he'd be back, unload the big load, do the chores, have a good hot supper, and be off to bed. Later in early spring the neighbor came with his sawing outfit and other neighbors came to help cut the wood into cord length – four foot lengths. Then came the job of loading the wood and taking it to town where it was piled in freight cars. A cord which was 8' x 4' x 4' was sold for $2.00 a cord. This gave us enough money to buy a gang plow with two plow shares."[10]

Mary Pauls, Peter's niece and former Glenbush resident, described this house as a building smaller than even a log cabin. Maria had never seen this house before, as it had been a bachelor's house. Together they changed this bachelor's pad into a comfortable home for two.

One of the things she had to contend with was bedbugs. They got rid of the bedbugs that came from the plaster walls by spreading some form of powder along the floor. On another occasion she found a nest of mice in her feather bed. How does a young bride who has moved from a home of many people to a log house in the bush where she might know very few people survive? Peter's two sisters, Margaret and Sara, helped her along and made her feel at home as much as possible. Once again she became involved in church activities, playing the piano for the church choir and teaching Sunday school.

A few weeks after their wedding, the newlyweds received a letter from Maria's mother indicating that they had received a good report from Ella and Isaac Block who had apparently gone to Glenbush and visited them. One of the sentences that stood out in this particular letter was, "the piano is silent and Maria's voice is no longer audible." During the time that Maria lived at home were days filled with music. Her mother missed that sound.

Maria's days were busy but quiet. She did not have a radio or a piano at her Glenbush home at that time. Everything had to be prepared from scratch. Food (vegetables and some meat) had to be canned due to the fact that there were no freezers. They did have an ice cellar, which was a 6 x 6 x 6 foot hole. Over this was erected a shingled roof which kept the cellar cool. Slanting from north to south, with the north side almost touching the ground, the roof was covered with moss. One entered this tiny house by a small door on the south side. In this fashion things could be kept cold in the summer. In the winter they dipped the meat in ice water, which preserved it until it was prepared for eating.

To have fresh meat each week, they were part of a beef ring in which they would butcher an animal and cut it up. The farmer whose turn it was to deliver the animal would come the following morning, load the meat into his buggy, and deliver the meat to the various homes in the ring. They operated this ring for about 10 years. In this way they always had fresh meat and everyone involved would get the best meat cuts. Maria also churned her own butter and did all her own sewing on a treadle sewing machine. In addition to this, it was not uncommon for the women to help with the outdoor chores.

One of the things that she had indicated to Peter in letters was that she wanted a big family – 15 children in all. By February of 1935 she was expecting her first child. How does a pioneer wife prepare for the coming of a new child? Baby showers were unheard of, times were tough, and money was tight. Everything was prepared ahead of time by the new mother to be. She was responsible for making all her own little baby nightgowns, flannel diapers, blankets, etc. from patterns that she made herself. Women did not have access to vitamins so there was no prenatal care available. Maria was basically responsible for her own physical health making sure that she ate right. The depression was particularly hard on pregnant women because food was often very scarce. In some parts when there was no food to be had they ate the weeds. Farming is hard work by nature. By October of 1935, she had not gained as much weight as she should have and was considered to be thin and underweight thus developing complications. Her first baby was born in a hospital in Saskatoon on October 16, 1935.

They named their daughter Lily Florence - after a flower and renowned nurse Florence Nightingale who had made a name for herself tending the sick and injured. Peter was also in the hospital during the time for some surgery. Because of complications in Maria's pregnancy, his surgery was postponed until she was out of danger. When both parents were well again, they traveled back to Glenbush together to start life as a family of three.

The care of a newborn during the depression was challenging. There were no disposable diapers in existence at that time, and the average newborn goes through 80 to 90 diapers per week. She had to wash her diapers each day to be ready for all the changes that a baby needed. Diapers were boiled in hot water to prevent the wet urine smell from appearing in the home. Dirty diapers were boiled over and over until they were clean, and then they would then be hung to dry. If a clean diaper was needed and none was quite dry, they would hang them on the door of the wood stove to dry faster. Over the years she often had two babies in diapers at the same time. Peter's older sister, Sara, only had eight diapers that were rotated over and over again. During the early years, Peter and Maria spent much time at the Pauls' house, which was three miles away. Maria would help with the cooking in the home, and in turn Nicolai & Sara's oldest daughter, twelve-year-old Mary, would help the Wiens with their laundry. Every Monday Mary would walk to the Wiens farm to help with the washing and ironing, then walk back home on Tuesday. To Mary, Maria was the big sister she never had. Mary simply loved her Aunt Maria. Another service that Mary did for her Aunt was to sew some dresses for her. Once Mary asked her if she could sew a different kind of dress for her. Maria declined the offer saying, "Auch, what do I need another dress for when I'm pregnant all the time anyways?" So Mary just sewed another maternity dress.

During the depression, the size of families decreased. In Canada, the birth rate dropped from 13.1 live births per 100 in 1930 to 9.7 in 1937. Records show that the Derksen family added 39 babies to their clan during the 30's. Peter and Maria contributed by bringing 4 new babies into the world – Lily (1935), Herbert Peter (September 25 of 1937), Rose Hildegard (November 3 of 1938), and Anna Grace (November 6 of 1939). The last two were only 1 year and 3 days apart. Herb and Rose were born at the Rabbit Lake hospital while Anna was born at home and delivered into the world by a midwife.

The depression was hard on Saskatchewan farmers. Many people left the city to find jobs on the farms in exchange for room and board. Southern Saskatchewan was hit harder than the north, partly because they experienced dust bowl storms. At this time they still did not have soil erosion programs in place. Dust storms would roll in and remove all of the topsoil that may have been seeded that day and the farmer would have to start all over again with his seeding. In 1937 the wheat crop was so bad that it wasn't worth taking to the elevator. Although wheat sold at $1.02 per bushel, the crop yield was 2.6 bushels per acre. Many farmers pooled their wheat and took it to the mills to be ground into flour, which would take them through until next years crop when hopefully it would be better. On top of the loss of soil and water, the Canadian farmers also experienced years of drought and grasshoppers that came in and destroyed what little crops were planted. With wheat prices so low farmers started planting new crops such as oats, rye, flax, and alfalfa that adapted better to the dry climate. They also used different tilling methods, crop rotations, and artificial fertilizer. This helped to increase the productivity of the fields by the end of the 30's.

One of the best lessons learned from the Great Depression doing without or making due with what you had. In order to make that work, people had to get along and live in peace with each other. One example of this was the beef ring. By sharing the animal, no family went without fresh meat and eventually received each part of beef to feed their families. If one neighbor's cow was dry and another's was fresh, the family would share the milk or the butter with the family whose cow was not able to produce these items. Each family looked after the needs of their neighbor. Glenbush families also received some governmental relief in the form of fish, cheese, and clothing. The fish was reported to be so salty that it needed to be soaked for a day or so before it was palatable. The government often used the local church as the distribution center for passing out relief to the families in the area. The clothing that churches received was also doled out to the various families. When Maria received a piece of clothing that might be too big for her children, she took it apart, washed it, and used the reverse side of the material for a new garment for her children or herself. Much of this clothing came in the form of material from gunnysacks or 100 lb. flour sacks. Nothing was thrown out. Even the cuffs from worn out socks were used to make mittens.

Everything was made by hand – even their laundry soap and candles. Candles were made from tallow wax together with a fine piece of cotton that served as a wick. In this manner the Glenbush and Borden people were able to survive the depression years – not by hoarding stuff for their own use or saving it for another day, but by sharing what they had with their neighbors.

The following are examples of some recipes Maria used during the Depression Era.

Poor Man's Pudding

Combine: 1/3 c. brown sugar   ] Spread in a
            1 c. flour   ] baking pan.
            1 t. baking powder   ]
            Pinch salt   ]
            ½ c milk   ]
Mix: 1 c. brown sugar   ] Pour over batter and
            2 c. hot water   ] bake at 350F
            1 T. butter   ] for ½ hour.
            ½ t. nutmeg   ]

Making Your Own Laundry Soap

6 lbs clean grease (pig's lard), strained
1 can lye
5 cups soft water
2 T. borax
2T sugar
½ cup ammonia

Melt fat in a large iron or enamel pan or cauldron (no aluminum). Cool grease to 80 F and combine 13 oz. can of lye with 5 cups of water in enamel pan stirring slowly with long wooden paddle. Long paddle is necessary to keep from splashing hands. Cool to 70F. Add lye water gradually to fat, stirring slowing for 10 min. Stir until mixture is creamy and then add borax, sugar and ammonia. Mix well and pour into shallow pans or cardboard box. Cool slowly for 24 hours. Remove from mold and cut with string into bars. Stack and let dry for two weeks. If properly dried, soap should be white and will float.

- Stories and Recipes of the Great Depression of the 1930's
Compiled by Rita Van Amber

Klopps (Hamburgers) for larger groups
This was Maria's recipe for hamburgers.

Five pounds of ground beef
Almost the same amount in volume of shredded potatoes
Half this amount of chopped or thinly sliced and chopped onions
Six eggs
One tablespoon of salt
One teaspoon of pepper
Four heaping tablespoons of flour
Four teaspoons of Baking Powder
One cup of cream

Mix ingredients with your hands, heat oil in a pan or two
Spoon into the pan and flatten them to make them spread out and fry on both sides.

Chapter 14

Taking the Good with the Bad-
The Wiens Family during World War II

Hate Reveals its Ugly Face – The Circumstances of World War II

Proverbs 6:16-19
"Here are six things God hates, and one more that he loathes with a passion:"

"Arrogant eyes"	"A lying tongue"	"Feet that race down a wicked track"
	A Heart that hatches evil plots	
"A mouth that lies under oath"	"Hands killing the innocent"	"A troublemaker in the home"

   While the rest of the world was lying 'fallow' in a state of depression, there was one person who was quietly making a name for him, sowing the seeds of discontentment among his fellow citizens. Adolf Hitler was the founder and leader of the Nazi Party, a ruthless Reich Chancellor, and the guiding force of the Third Reich from 1933 to 1945. He was also the Head of State and Supreme Commander of the Armed Forces. In short he was a dictator who believed the Germans were the master race and part of the pure Aryan race supremacy. His agenda was to break up the Versailles Treaty that was agreed upon at the end of WW1, to rid the world of his number one enemy – the Jews, and to establish the Germans as the supremacy of the Aryan race. On September first of 1939 Hitler invaded Poland, whose independence was guaranteed by Britain and France. This prompted a declaration of war on Germany from Britain and Canada, and started World War II. Over the course of the next years, problems escalated and more countries became involved. In 1941 Canada declared war on Japan, and Germany invaded Russia. In 1945 the United States declared war on Japan and Germany and entered the war on the side of the Allies. With a strong Allied army against Hitler, the threads of the Nazi regime started to unravel. Gradually, Hitler lost the confidence of his followers and began a slow withdrawal from the world making fewer and fewer appearances in public. He was completely defeated in 1945.

Map of Europe in the 1920s

Interwar Europe

Europe in 1937:

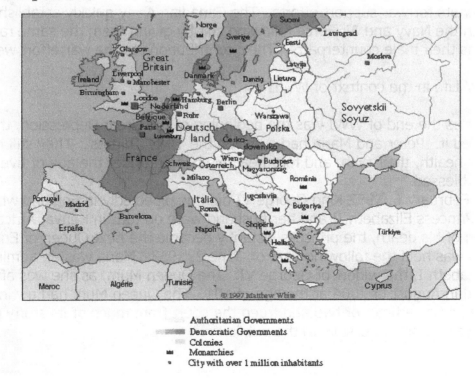

Authoritarian Governments
Democratic Governments
Colonies
Monarchies
City with over 1 million inhabitants

Canada and World War II

During the years that World War II was in progress, Canada had much to be proud of in their contributions to the war. Canada entered the war on September 10, 1939 sending troops to England to defend the coastline of the United Kingdom and eventually took part in the battles of Dieppe (1942), and Italy (1944). They were involved in the invasion of Normandy on June 6, 1944 taking Caen and advancing along the seacoast to Pas-de-Calais and ultimately defeating Germany at Dieppe in September of 1942. At the time of their entry into World War II, Canada was hardly prepared. Their army was small and the few weapons they had were outdated. Between 1939 and 1945, to their credit, Canada put together the largest army in its history – 750,000 men and women in uniform.

The supporters on the home front also acted quickly. Factories that had once created the luxuries such as lipstick and stockings were turned into war factories turning out guns, ships, planes, and military vehicles sending more than half of these products directly to Europe. Children and mothers collected cardboard and milk bottle caps, gave up icing on cakes, and entered the world of hoarding anything that could be used in the war effort. Many of these factories were run and managed by women who stepped to the plate so that the men could go and fight for freedom.

The Canadian Women's Army Corps (WAC) was formed in 1941 upon the realization that eventually the army would need more workers and the fact that women were pressuring the government to be allowed to join the Armed Forces. Until this time, all the efforts on behalf of the women of Canada were resisted. That changed when the British Air Ministry suggested that they send their Women's Auxiliary Air Forces (WAAF) over to Canada's Royal Air Force training bases to train and prepare the female recruits for war support efforts. The Canadian Army quickly established the WAC's with the Navy and Air Force following suit by giving them the same ranks and uniforms as their male counterparts. Their contributions to the war effort were great.

The Wiens' Life in the context of WWII

Just as the end of WWI was the beginning of the Great Depression, the start of WWII ended it. Peter and Maria had survived the 'Dirty Thirties'. They still had their farm, their health, their faith, and four healthy children under the age of five. They were truly blessed.

On February 6, 1952 King George VI died unexpectedly in England while his daughter Princess Elizabeth II and her husband were on tour in Kenya, Africa. Upon notification of his death, the princess instantly became the next Queen of England. Her coronation was held the following year on June 2, 1953. Maria was an admirer of Queen Elizabeth I, the widow of George VI. The Queen Mum, as she was affectionately called, died in August of 2004 at the age of 101. The Queen Mum had a winning smile, bet on the horses a time, or two and freed the court from much of its stuffy protocol making royalty more accessible to the public.

With Hitler's war raging in Europe, farmers were once again called upon to feed the armies in Europe. One of the biggest problems farmers and the Canadian Wheat Board had to deal with was an oversupply of wheat that came with improved farming methods and better crops. During the 40's and 50's, wheat prices were still considered low even though farming methods had greatly improved, and farms were becoming larger in size.

While the farmers were growing bigger crops, the Wiens family was also getting bigger. Every year or so, a new baby would make its appearance. After the war was over in 1946, a full basement was dug with a two-story structure added onto the house to create more badly needed space. Up until that time they had lived in a space that consisted of only five rooms. Just as the rooms of The White House in Washington, D.C. had names such as the Oval Office, Lincoln Room, Blue Room, and the Red Room the Wiens family also had unofficial names for the various rooms in their home. These included the Blue Room, the Boys' room and the Girls' room. Until the addition of the house was built, Peter and Maria slept in The Blue Room. During the early years while the children were in the baby stage, they slept in various cribs or boxes on the floor. As the children got older, they slept crosswise in the same bed in the living room. The only distinction in that room was dividers, such as sheets, that were put up to break it into sections. They had a cellar underneath the kitchen floor. This is where they kept their canned goods and milk cold. To access their stored food in the cellar, they had to climb down a ladder. The kitchen also doubled as the dining room. There was little or no privacy in the house but they were very cozy.

When they added on the new section, they had another five rooms in which to spread their wings. They added two rooms – a bedroom for the parents and an official living room downstairs, plus three bedrooms upstairs. Until the upper level was completely finished some years later, the children who slept upstairs got a taste of 'camping'. Plywood was not used in Glenbush at this time, but they used loose boards to walk on and the bedsprings were placed across the bare joists. From this vantage point they could see the stars, if the roof wasn't all frosted in. Beth recalled an incident that occurred before the upper level was complete. One day she was taking a nap in this space when she saw a mouse crawl up the side, look around, and climb back down.

When it got to be too cold they moved their blankets downstairs and slept on the dining room table until their beds were brought down the next day. This probably lasted two or more winters. Maria remembered these as the winters when not one of her children got sick. Until a furnace was installed, the Wiens home was heated with a pot-bellied stove, which needed to be tended very carefully. On one occasion someone put in wood that started a chimney fire. They quickly had to dismantle the pipes and put them in the snow to put out the fire. Such a fire was usually started because of the oil built up in the pipes by burning green or uncured wood. Green wood on its own would not burn hot enough to start a fire but if they burned enough green wood over a period of time, the oil in the wood tar built up in the chimney pipes. Then when they built a hot fire with dry wood this oil could catch fire and generate a tremendous amount of heat.

Nowadays, families tend to give their children their own rooms. For the Wiens family, this was not a luxury they could afford. In most cases, two to five people shared the rooms. Two of the rooms upstairs had two beds in each of the rooms. Only the oldest of the bunch might be so fortunate as to have their own room, and this did not happen until the family size was substantially smaller.

The decade of the 40's was filled with high points and low points, changes and adjustments. One of Maria's favorite verses was Psalms 121:1 - "I will lift up my eyes unto the hills from whence cometh my help. My help comes from the Lord, the Maker of heaven and earth." (KJV). The year 1944 stands out as being a low point for Peter and Maria. It would be best described as a year of catastrophe with one setback after another. Their faith was severely tried. The Wiens' now had a family of 7 children to support and baby Beth was on the way. That year their crops were exceptionally poor and Peter didn't know how he was ever going to support his family. During the drought years they purchased a pure bred Holstein calf for $10.00, which was a lot of money at that time, only to lose her later while she was calving. Six months later, half of their crops were destroyed by hail. While farmers can expect this to happen from time to time, it appeared to hit only their quarter of land. Because crop insurance only started in 1939, it is doubtful that they had crop insurance. They got an average of about 15 bushels per acre while their neighbors harvested a good crop. With that source of income just about wiped out, they turned to raising chickens as their main income. Maria received a $50.00 gift from her mother and they decided to invest this money in buying chickens.

An innovative pioneer, Peter wasn't afraid to try anything once - although the neighbors thought this to be a rather foolish notion. They purchased 500 little chickens from a hatchery in Saskatoon with the intention of selling the eggs back to the hatchery in the spring. During the remainder of the year, they would sell the eggs to the local creamery. The hatchery paid about three times more than the creamery. The chickens had to be purebred with a very specific procedure. In the fall a hatchery representative came to test and cull the hens, tagging every hen, and in return the hatchery would pay them $.60 per dozen eggs. Peter's job was to separate the high quality eggs from those that weren't. This process was referred to as culling. Cull was done by candling, which meant that each egg had to be held up to a candle to see how fresh it was. This would also show if the egg had blood spots or any other imperfections. The eggs were then weighed to see if they were small, medium, or large. Before all this was done, they had to be washed and dried by hand. Rose and Anna had this job. Then they packed the eggs in paper trays that held 30 eggs each. These trays were piled one of top of each other in an egg crate or box.

In December even this source of income was almost wiped out as well. A few days before Christmas, early in the morning, the chicken barn caught fire. No one had telephones at that time so it was up to Peter and Maria to do what they could to save the chickens. They chased the chickens to the other end of the barn and threw them out the window. Unfortunately they just jumped right back into the barn and were burned. Out of the original 500 chickens only 50 were saved. One thing that should be noted here is that when a one neighbor needed assistance, other neighbors would be there to help them in every way possible. After Christmas, the neighbors came to help rebuild the barn. Despite all of their reversals they had food on the table, clothes on their backs, and the strength to start over – all without the assistance of welfare or government assistance. Peter was ready to give up and leave the area but Maria stood by him and told him "No, Peter, the Lord has brought us this far and HE will see us through this as well". Maria took God at His promise and truly "tested" the word of God, which was her anchor, and found that it was good. (Ps. 34:8). Her faith was strengthened by this difficult test.

Despite that setback, that Christmas turned out to be very special. Peter had hidden her Christmas present in the barn and ran in to get it. What was special about that particular gift was not the plaque itself but what was written on it. This plaque hidden in the barn had survived the fire that destroyed everything else. As Maria summed up, that year God got them through that difficult time. They always had food on the table, and clothes on their backs.

Romans 8:28   the plaque Maria received for Christmas in 1944

This plaque remained on her living room wall in every place that she lived as a reminder of God's provision to her.

If 1944 proved to be a breaking and/or turning point in their lives, there were other years that served as high points. Seven children were born to Peter and Maria in the 40's – Reuben Peter (November 14 of 1940), Edward Peter (April 4 of 1942), Violet Viola (April 13 of1943), Elizabeth (Beth) Helen (March 26 of 1945), John Peter (May 17 of 1946), Victor Peter (January 10 of 1948), and Gerhard (George) Peter (February 10 of 1949). Each child she welcomed as a gift and blessing from the Lord. None were an intrusion in her life. Despite the smallness of the home, Peter continually told her that there was always room for one more.

In 1941 she sent her firstborn child out the door to the Artichoke school. Education was equally important to Peter and Maria. Peter served as a trustee for the Artichoke District. Because the school bus did not make its appearance in the area until the 50's, parents were responsible for providing their own transportation to and from school. Glenbush did not have a high school. Peter Enns, seven years older than Lily and a high school student, came to live with the Wiens household and help them out. He would take Lily and Herb to school in a horse and buggy and pick up the neighbor children along the way.

During the 1940's, seven of their children got their start in the Artichoke school. Peter Wiens served in community activities, including a term as a trustee for the Artichoke School district. Another year, Marie Enns (Peter Enns' sister) lived with them, caring for the children and going to high school until Lily and Herb were old enough to handle the horses and sleigh by themselves. For three years, they worked together with their neighbors, Jake and Mary Klassen, getting the children to and from school. Later on, when Beth was the baby, Peter's niece (Marie Enns) lived with them so that she too could attend high school. The reason for this was that there was no high school close to the Enns farm.

Christmas of 1942 also stood out in Maria's memory. Peter was a person who loved to surprise his wife, and he knew that she missed having a piano at home, so he sold five hogs in order to buy her a piano of her own. On December 24, as she told the story, he was very excited and also very busy. He had taken a load of pigs to town to sell that day. That night after all the children were dressed and ready to go to church for the Christmas Eve program, she had to put the house in order but she didn't know why. When they got to church that night, people asked her what she was getting for Christmas. She told them that she had no idea but they all knew what it was. It was the best-kept secret in Glenbush that season. When they arrived home, there was the big upright piano standing against the living room wall. What a surprise that was for her. She had that piano until 1966 when she sold it in the farm auction to Reuben Derksen, a relative in Borden who still owns it to this day. After Reuben and Elizabeth Derksen had this piano, a tuner told them this piano was built in the 1800's and offered to rebuild it for them so that it would hold its tune better. Unfortunately they regretted doing this.

Peter was also a good mechanic. He had taken a course in mechanics in Winnipeg, which enabled him to fix his machinery as well as help others to fix theirs. Being the first to buy a tractor with steel rims, he was able to use it to his advantage. With this tractor, a trade was bartered that benefited everyone involved. They had a breaking plow but there were many trees that needed to be cleared off the land. To help each other out, the neighbors would come and chop down the trees while Peter broke their land. A breaking plow, also known as a bush plow, has a number of plow shares with a sharp knife-like blade in front of the shares. This knife cuts through the soil so that the shares can go deeper into the ground. The shares, which have a flat piece of iron at the bottom to strengthen it and keep the shares from breaking, then turn over the soil or sod. It can also cut through small trees, shrubs or stumps. Peter and Maria had one of the biggest John Deere tractors in the area. Not so much by choice but by what was available. When people started to drive cars, the community started a snowplough club and invested in a snowplough, which was attached to Peter's tractor. It then became his responsibility to keep the roads open during the winter.

Perhaps because of the availability of tractors and better machinery, by 1949 crops were greatly improved. It was in this year that they got their first pull type combine, which was traded two years later for a new self-propelled one. This was a big and expensive machine. In order to pay for the combine, Peter would do custom combining for the neighbors and surrounding districts. This combine remained in use until 1966 when it was sold at the farm auction.

In 1949 Peter traded in his used car for a brand new, blue, two door Ford. Incidentally that old car he had traded in did more than just take his family to and from church. It also did double duty as his 'truck', hauling calves in the back. To accommodate this process, he would remove the back seat and place a box in the back, ensuring the warmth of the young calves. Help someone with a cementing job? No problem. He strapped the wheelbarrow on the top of the car, put the cement mixer in the back of the car, and off he'd go.

During the 50's the baby boom was in full swing. It was estimated that there were 11,000 babies born a day. As these baby boomers started school, new schools in United States and Canada could not be built fast enough. In 1953 the school attendance rose by two million. Peter and Maria had three more children in the 50's – Naomi Ruth (April 3 of 1951), Melita Margaret (January 8 of 1953) and Blondina (Dina) Johanna (November 4 of 1954). Of all the babies only six were born in a hospital. The rest were born at home with either Peter, a midwife or a doctor delivering the babies. All of the children from Anna to George were born at home. Naomi was born in Saskatoon, Melita and Blondina were born in Rabbit Lake. By the time Maria was carrying Blondina, with a due date in October, she was getting well past her due date and had still not delivered. After thirteen births, her stomach muscles had weakened considerably and the doctor told Maria that she was plumb worn out. Maria responded by telling the doctor that the baby would come when she was good and ready and she would have to be patient.

The Wiens family experienced many changes during the 50's. The 50's represented the maturing and nest leaving years for some of the children and a beginning of life for others. In the spring of 1951 there were three teenagers, one preteen, four between the ages of six and twelve, three between two and six, and one in the cradle. Some of the children started to leave home to work elsewhere or go on for further education. Lily was the first to leave in 1953 to attend Bethany Bible School in Hepburn for a year before returning home to help again. In the summer of 1956 the Artichoke school closed its doors. Students who attended there were sent to the consolidated school in the town of Glenbush. During the last year that Artichoke operated as a school, Herb's education was interrupted due to a lack of teachers. Herb attended Bethany Bible School for one winter and then came back to finish his senior year in Glenbush during the 1956-57 school year. He graduated from Glenbush High School along with his sister Rose. During the year of 1956, Peter and Maria packed lunches for 10 children with Herb being the oldest child and George the youngest. There were no hot lunches for school children in those days. It was also necessary for all the families in the community to arrange for their own transportation to school until the school district started using a school bus in 1958. This was not a problem for the Wiens. The children used the Bennett wagon pulled by two horses and usually picked up various neighbors along the way.

At least once a year, Peter and Maria would go to Borden to visit her relatives. Each time they went they would take some of the children along, leaving the rest behind to do the chores and take care of the younger ones. At other times of the year, the Borden relatives would come to Glenbush. The year of 1956 was a time of change and adventure. Peter's sister and brother-in-law (Nick and Sara Pauls) together with their two remaining children at home (Jake and Nick) moved away from Glenbush for the warmer climate in B.C. John and Margaret Enns had already pulled out in 1948 for Ontario but first settled in Elm Creek, Manitoba where John's brother was living. The Enns completed their move to Ontario a few years later.

In June of 1956, Peter and Maria together with Reuben, Beth, and Anna traveled to Elm Creek for the double wedding of Marie and Sue Enns. Care of the farm was left in the hands of the next oldest in line, Herb and Rose. Whether it was planned ahead of time or whether it was a spur of the moment decision is not known. Peter accompanied by Maria sang a song *Die Unschult Bringt Freude.'* Loosely translated into English the title means "The Innocence Brings Joy". Their trips were never long but they were a much-needed break for Peter and Maria from farm life and all its responsibilities.

Meal preparations were all made by hand with the cooking and baking done on a wood stove. In order to keep the stove supplied with wood, the children would have to bring in enough to fill the wood box beside the stove. Before running water was put in the house, the water was pumped and brought in one bucket at a time. In the winter they would fill a galvanized tub with clean snow and melt it on the stove. Even when the family had running water, they still had to heat the water on the stove before dishes could be washed. Nothing was thrown away without using it twice- even the dishwater was thrown outside to water the plants.

Early pioneers kept their homes lit with kerosene lamps. The lamps used in the Wiens home were glass with a clear dome that would need to be washed on a regular basis. Because it got dark early, the men took a lantern out to the barn so that they could see what they were doing.

Doing laundry for such a large family was a big effort. Maria would keep Anna or Rose home on a Monday so that they could get the laundry done faster. Maria had a wringer washing machine that could do damage to the human arm if a person got their arm caught in the wringers. The water was so hot that you could see the steam rising from it. After a load of laundry was washed, they hung the sheets and clothes on a wash line outside. In the winter the clothing on the line would freeze solid.

A benefit of hanging the laundry out to dry was that it had a nice outdoor fresh smell. Once the clothes were dry, they were brought inside, sprinkled with water, and rolled up to get ready for ironing, which was another major task. Maria had two 'sad' irons. One would be in use by the person doing the ironing and the other would be heating up on the stove. In this way, they could keep ironing without interruption. What is a 'sad' iron, you say? Why did they call it by that name? In 1871, a housewife, Mrs. Mary Potts, filed her first patent on her iron. She believed that when the body of the iron, which was made from cast iron, was filled with a non-conductive heat material such as plaster of Paris, cement, or clay it would hold the heat longer so that more garments could be ironed without reheating. The sad iron was designed with a detachable handle. In this manner, the housewife doing her ironing could carry the cold iron to the stove, remove the handle and attach it to the hot iron. It was called the 'sad' iron because ironing was viewed as such a sad and hot drudgery job.

Electricity did not come to the community until the 1950's. Around the mid-fifties, Peter was selected to go from farm to farm to ask his neighbors whether or not they would like to have electricity brought into the area. To do this, he used a variety of travel methods. When the roads were blocked, he resorted to skiing from place to place. The first electric lights came on during dinnertime in 1957 and kerosene lamps were retired.

While the farmers worked hard, they also made time for recreation. The Glenbush Agricultural Society would put on an annual fair in order to attract more people into their circle of activities. One year they put on a small circus with a Ferris wheel, a merry-go-round, and other rides. Another year, they had an airplane at the fair that would take passengers in the air for 15 minutes for a fee. There was a raffle drawn and the lucky winner got a free ride. Peter drew the lucky ticket and got his ride in a plane. He had never been in a plane before that or after that.

On July 1, 1959 Peter and Maria celebrated their Silver Wedding. With so many relatives present for this celebration, Maria did all of the cooking and set up an eating area in the garage to feed everyone. Maria bought or sewed new dresses for all the girls. It was on a warm Sunday afternoon, with the two youngest girls (Blondina and Melita) serving as flower girls, that Maria and Peter walked up the aisle to give thanks to God for 25 years together. They remembered both the good times and the hard times. Little did they know that they would only have just a little over two more years together before one of them would be taken from the marriage union.

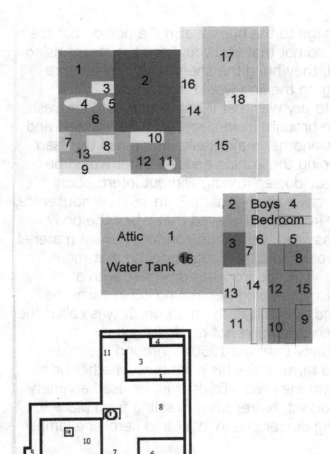

Farmhouse floor plan

Lower level:
Blue Room (1)
Dining Room (2)
Pantry – later on the
     Bathroom (6)
Kitchen (13)
Entry Way (12)
Parent's room (17)
Living Room (15)

Upper Level:
Boys Room (7)
Girls room (14)
Girls room (15)

Cellar:
Cold Room (3)
Cistern (10)
Potato Bin (6)
Wood stored here (8)
Furnace (1)

Above: butter churn, wood heater, indoor kerosene lamps
(the lamps that the Wiens home had were all clear glasss)

an indoor toilet (the family would have to empty the bucket inside this one – indoor flushing toilets did not exist)

A mangle - sheets and pants were ironed on this mangle by means of rolling the item into mangle

egg beater

Top row: sad iron, meat grinder – meat was ground up in this kitchen tool to make ground beef;

Middle row: (Left)an older washing machine, (Center)wash board – dirty clothes were first rubbed on this in hot water before they went into the washing machine. (Right)All the family pictures were taken with a brownie camera such as this. When family pictures were sent to the relatives in Russia, the parents dressed the children up in real old looking clothes so that the people in Russia didn't get any ideas of how affluent people in Canada were. It also insured that the family actually received the picture in question.

Bottom left : A barn lantern

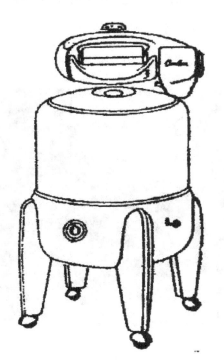

Top: a picture of a mother rubbing dirty clothes on a wash board.

Bottom: a gas operated washing machine that preceeded the electric washing machine.

Farming methods

Seeding
1930

It's haying
Time!

Combining Time
Peter bought this combine in 1951

Peter was an avid reader. This habit
was instilled in his children, and eventually
passed it onto his grandchildren.

Chester's House — garage
sheepbarn
barn/silo outhouse house — garden
driveway ice house/tool shed — patatoe patch
graineries raspberry patch—

Above: An aerial view of the farm

Right: Peter Wiens with his friend and neighbor, Jake Klassen.

Jake was a bachelor in the area during the same time that Peter was. They did many things together before they married. Jake and Mary Klassen lived about half a mile away. Jake was in his 90's when he died in 2002.

Left: Rose and Anna cleaning eggs getting them ready for the market.

This is the way the pioneers traveled in the winter. The caboose the Wiens family had sat on sleds AND had a heater in it to keep everyone warm. The front of the caboose had two holes through it where the harness of the horses went through. Those were the Days!!!

This was Peter's first tractor. Notice that it has no rubber tires. It was ideal for breaking land. Peter was the first in the area to get a tractor and would break other farmer's land in exchange for other services.

Life was not all work on the farm.

Anna, Violet, Edward, and Reuben enjoy the sandbox by the house

This is the piano that Maria got in 1942 Melita and Naomi are having a go at the keys.

Maria was very creative with the snow wear of her children. This snowsuit was made by Maria for four-year-old Naomi in 1955

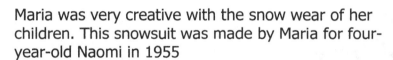

Even Maria took time out to read to her children.

I wonder what she is reading to George and Naomi here.

The four youngest children:

Back row: L to R: George, Naomi
Front row: Melita and Blondina 1955

Glenbush would have evangelical meetings. One of the speakers in 1951 was Mr. C. N. Hiebert. Mr. Hiebert is holding Naomi with George standing beside.

These two pictures are of George before and after a haircut.
Notice the porch outside of the house. It was the responsibility of one of the children to sweep and wash it to keep the mud from coming in.

Some of the Wiens Children in the '50's and '60's

Top row: Blondina, Melita & Naomi
Middle row: George, John & Ed
Bottom row: Beth, Lily & Anna

July 1,1959

Peter and Maria Wiens'
Silver Wedding

The Wiens
Family:
Back Row L to R: Lily,
Reuben, Herb, Ed,
Rose and Vi
Middle Row: Anna,
Beth, John, Vic and
George
Front Row: Naomi,
Maria, Blondina,
Peter and Melita

Maria & Peter Wiens
With Maria's oldest brother &
his wife,
George and Justina Derksen

Silver Wedding Reception:

Peter & Maria Wiens
Next to them are Isaac and
Elizabeth Willems, her brother-
in-law and older sister.

Elizabeth met Isaac at Maria's
wedding in 1934!

Maria's Brothers and Sisters

Henry and Hulda (Klassen) Derksen (left) born May 31, 1915). Henry was born on November 12, 1914 in Canada. A farmer all his life, he lived in Borden. After retirement they moved to Saskatoon.
Henry died on January 20, 2002. Hulda is currently living in Abbotsford, B.C.

Tina (right) was the first Derksen child to be born in Canada. Born on July 17, 1907, she had aspirations to be a nurse but family finances did not permit this dream to come to reality. She married a local Bordonite, Frank Peters (born June 23, 1903) in Borden on January 16, 1930 at the beginning of the Great Depression. Frank and Tina lived in Saskatoon, Terrace where he was involved in the logging business. Frank died on December 31, 1980; Tina outlived him by 13 years passing away on November 11, 1993.

Elizabeth (right) was born in Russia on January 12, 1901. She married Isaac Williems (born November 7, 1896) on February 28, 1935.
After they retired from farming in Waldheim, they moved to Saskatoon.

Isaac and Elizabeth never had children but spent much time with the nieces and nephews. Isaac died on August 1, 1979. Elizabeth outlived him by 20 years passing away on March 6, 2000.

Isaac and Elizabeth always had time for those who came to visit them – even unannounced.

Anna (top left and top right) was born in Russia on January 15, 1895. She married
Peter J. Rempel (top left) (born June 4, 1888) on March 18, 1915. Peter died on
August 29, 1928 as a result of an injury sustained some years earlier. Anna married
Henry Block (born January 2, 1895) on May 18, 1930. The Rempel-Blocks were farmers
in the Borden area. Anna died on December 21, 1947. Henry married Elizabeth Froese
on June 18, 1949. Henry died on January 11, 1956. A seamstress, Elizabeth Froese
Block (born March 29, 1901) died October 31, 1994.

Ella, (right) the first Derksen child to finish 8th grade
was born on November 19, 1909 in Canada. She
married Isaac Block (born May 24, 1905) on June 8,
1930. Isaac was born in Russia. A farmer in the
Borden area, he was also one of the preachers in the
Borden M.B. Church.

They retired to Saskatoon after being done with
farming. Isaac died from heart failure on March 20,
1997. Ella followed seven months later on October
26, 1997.

George Derksen was born in Russia on Sept. 17, 1892. He married Maria Unger (top left) (born Aug. 10, 1893) on Nov. 24, 1913. A farmer, George & Maria moved to B.C. where the weather was warmer. Maria died on Jan. 31, 1949. George married Justina Siemens (born March 13, 1898) on April 30, 1949. George died on February 15, 1962. Justina passed away on May 24, 1984.

Margaret (left) was born in Russia February 6, 1903. She married John Stobbe (born July 18, 1902) (below) on February 2, 1924. John was the preacher and Margaret was the singer. Margaret died on February 15, 1944. John married Susie Hiebert (born Oct. 29, 1906) (below) on Sept. 24, 1944. John died on September 5, 1976. Susie died on Nov. 17, 1992

Agnes Derksen with Jake Stobbe (left) was born in Russia on February 2, 1905. She was four months old when her parents immigrated to Canada. Agnes was the one to break traditions in the Derksen home. She was the first daughter to attend Bible School, wear a veil etc. She married Jacob Stobbe (born November 24, 1903 in Russia) on July 17, 1927. The Stobbes were farmers as well as deacons in the Borden church. Their retirement years were spent in Saskatoon. Jake died on September 24, 1977. They were married 50 years.

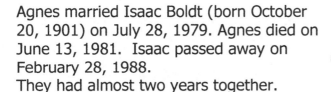

Agnes married Isaac Boldt (born October 20, 1901) on July 28, 1979. Agnes died on June 13, 1981. Isaac passed away on February 28, 1988.
They had almost two years together.

Susie (Susanna) Derksen was the last Derksen children. She was born in Canada on December 30, 1915. She married Jacob Hamm (born May 5, 1917) on October 27, 1940. Jake and Susie were farmers in the Borden area.
A farm accident in 1970 forced Jake to put more of the day-to-day farm work on the shoulders of his sons. Eventually the Hamm's retired to Saskatoon. Jake died on February 13, 2003.
As of this writing Susie is living in a retirement community in Saskatoon.

Justina Derksen (left) was born on August 16, 1893 in Russia. She was the first of ten daughters to be born to the Derksens. On November 24, 1912, she married Peter Bergman (born January 13, 1889). Farmers in the Borden area, they also gave the Derksens their first grandchild. The Bergmans only had girls.

Peter Bergman had thoroughbred horses on his farm but was forced to give them up when there was some disease found in his land that was killing his horses.

The Bergmans retired to Hepburn and eventually moved into a nursing home. Peter died on July 6, 1985. Justina outlived him by eight years living to the ripe old age of 100 passing away on December 20, 1993.

John J. Derksen (left) was born June 15, 1897 in Russia. He married Lena Odenbach (born August 18, 1897) on January 23, 1921. For a few years they farmed in the Borden area. Their first years of marriage were spent living in the old Diefenbaker shack. Interestingly enough, Lena had lived in this same shack aschild.

John and Lena were never blessed with children of their own. Therefore, they adopted two girls, Ruby and Helen. The Derksens retired to Abbotsford, B.C.

Here a passerby would notice the roses that grew in their yard.

Lena died November 22, 1988 after 67 years of marriage. John followed five months on June 14, 1989.

Sara Derksen was born on Jan. 23, 1899 in Russia. She married Paul Wiebe on June 19, 1921. Sara was instrumental in the salvation of Maria when she encouraged her to go to the church for help when Maria realized that she was a sinner.

Sara died on April 6, 1930 leaving behind two young boys, Alwin and Walter.

Paul (below) married Sara Balzer,(born March 3, 1905) on November 28, 1930. Paul and Sara eventually moved to British Columbia. During his working years, Paul was a schoolteacher in various locations of Saskatchewan. During that time, he was ordained to the ministry – a capacity he kept for many years. Paul died on August 24, 1989.

Sara Balzer Wiebe (below right) died on August 3, 1994.

Derksen children with their mother, Anna Derksen, at her 90th birthday
Left to Right: back row: John Derksen, Henry Derksen & George Derksen
Middle row: Ella Block, Agnes Stobbe, Elizabeth Willems, Maria Wiens
Front row: Susanna Hamm, Grandmother Derksen, Justina Bergman

The Derksen Aunts and Uncles at a family Reunion in 1980
Left to right: Isaac & Ella Block, Agnes Stobbe, Elizabeth Willems, Tina Peters, Henry & Hulda Derksen, Maria & Abe Martens

Maria with her sisters and brothers during the latter 1980's
   Back row: Abe Martens, Tina Peters, Elizabeth Willems, Hulda & Henry Derksen
   Front row: Maria Martens, Isaac & Ella Block, Susie & Jake H

Chapter 15

Maria's Music

Throughout the ages, music has always played a role. Regardless of the type of music, it is a tool to describe what was happening during a given time period in a person's life. It is used to sooth the ruffled soul and feed the mood of an individual. It is also a medium used to sing praises to God or an individual lover. Music was certainly central to Maria's life.

During the 1900's the world experienced a great variety of music, including the blues, folk, country, swing, jazz, rap, rock and roll, and heavy metal. Maria saw Elvis and the Beatles rise to fame. However, she never really listened to any of these genres. There was one kind of music that impacted her life in a big way – gospel songs - but she especially loved the hymns. My how she could pour her soul into the playing of those hymns. Many a time as she played them, they soothed her hurts and at the same time sang praise to God telling Him how much she loved Him. She loved so many of them. Here are examples of some of these songs that meant so much to Maria.

The early church worship service during the New Testament time was very liturgical – that is to say they followed a specific order with chanting and had its roots in scripture. Today's Roman Catholic Church has been following this order for nearly 2000 years. Their worship consisted of psalms sung from the Hebrew "Book of Praises". These were sung each day in one of two ways – antiphonal or responsorial chants. Antiphonal singing was when a group was divided into sections with one group singing to the other with a response coming from the second group. The responsorial chant was a method where the leader, accompanied by various instruments, would sing one line and wait for his congregation to sing the next line. Lines sung as a solo were called 'verses' and the congregational response was known as the 'response'. Here is one example:

O Gladsome Light, O Grace
By Louis Bourgeois, 1549 – translated by Robert Bridges 1895

1. O gladsome Light, O Grace
Of God the Father's Face,
The eternal splendor wearing;
Celestial, holy, blest,
Our Savior Jesus Christ,
Joyful in Thine appearing.

2. Now, ere day fadeth quite,

We see the evening light,
Our wonted hymn outpouring,
Father of might unknown,
Thee, His incarnate Son,
And Holy Ghost adoring.

3. To Thee of right belongs
All praise of holy songs,
O Son of God, Life-giver;
Thee, therefore, O Most High,
The world doth glorify
And shall exalt forever.

Isaac Watts (1674-1748), author of *Joy to the World and O God our Help in Ages Past,* started his compositions from the principle that the words should express the religious feelings of the people. John and Charles Wesley (1707-1788) carried this idea a step further, saying that both words and music should be written to "stir" the congregation, re-enforcing the notion that religious emotions play on the "feel good" factor. The Wesley's hymns were lively and active. The outcome of the "feel good" belief paid off. The Methodists congregations responded to their idea with vigor and enthusiasm. The enthusiasm of the Methodists drew many people from the established church to the Methodist Church. Charles Wesley published more than 4,500 hymns and left over 3,000 in manuscript form. Some of the Wesley hymns include *Christ the Lord is Risen Today, Jesus Lover of My Soul,* and *O For a Thousand Tongues.* The words to that hymn are as follows:

O For a Thousand Tongues to Sing

1.O for a thousand tongues to sing,
My great Redeemers praise,
The glories of my God and King,
The triumphs of his grace.

2. My gracious Master and my God,
Assist me to proclaim
To spread through the earth abroad,
The honors of Thy name.

3. Jesus! The name that charms our fears,
'Tis music in the sinners' ears,
That bids our sorrows cease,
'Tis life and health and peace.

4. He breaks the pow'r of cancelled sin,

He sets the prisoner free,
His blood can make the foulest clean –
His blood availed for me.

5. Hear Him, ye deaf; his praise ye dumb,
Your loosened tongues employ,
Ye blind, behold your Savior come;
And leap, ye lame, for joy.

Probably the most prolific hymnist in history was Fanny Crosby (1820-1915), the Queen of American writers. She wrote over 8,000 hymns, many of which are still in church hymnals. Her early life is riddled with tragedies. At the age of six weeks she was blinded when a quack doctor treated an eye infection incorrectly. Her father died a few months later, and her widowed 21- year -old mother hired herself out as a maid. She was greatly influenced by her mother, Eunice Crosby, who became her eyes by describing in great detail the world around her. Her grandmother read and explained the Bible to young Fanny, emphasizing the importance of prayer. The Crosbys' landlady, Mrs. Hawley, helped Fanny memorize the Bible –often she memorized five chapters a week. Self-pity was never in Fanny's vocabulary. Fanny's acceptance to her blindness is perhaps wrapped up in this little verse that she wrote at the age of eight:

Oh, what a happy child I am,
Although I cannot see!
I am resolved that in this world
Contented I will be!
How many blessings I enjoy
That other people don't!
So weep or sigh because I'm blind,
I cannot – nor I won't.[19]

Her music reached the masses and was used by D.L. Moody and Ira Sankey, drawing lost souls to the saving knowledge of the Savior. Some of her hymns include "*Blessed Assurance,*" "*All the Way the My Savior Leads Me*", "*To God Be the Glory*", "*Jesus, Keep Me Near the Cross*", and "*Safe in the Arms of Jesus*". Ironically, she was only paid one or two dollars for each poem she wrote and those who composed the tunes usually kept all the rights to the entire hymn.

On one occasion Fanny had a need for $5.00, not much money in our time but this represented a great deal of money in her time. Desperate for the needed funds, she did what she always did when she had a need – she turned to prayer. Within a few minutes, a stranger came to her door with the exact amount. Her first thought after this encounter was that how good it was that her Savior led her all the way. She wrote this hymn about that experience:

All the Way My Savior Leads Me

Written by Fanny J. Crosby; music by Robert Lowery
Based on Philippians 1:6; 3:10-15

All the way my Savior leads me-
What have I to ask beside?
Can I doubt His tender mercies,
Who through life has been my guide?
Heavenly peace, divinest comfort,
Here by faith in Him to dwell
For I know whate'er befalll me
Jesus doeth all things well.
For I know whate'er befalll me
Jesus doeth all things well.

All the way my Savior leads me-
Cheers each winding path I tread,
Gives me strength for every trial,
Feeds me with the living bread.
Though my weary steps may falter
And my soul a thirst may be
Gushing from the rock before me,
Lo! a spring of joy I see.
Gushing from the rock before me,
Lo! a spring of joy I see.

All the way my Savior leads me
Oh the fullness of His love!
Perfect rest in me is promised
In my Father's house above.
When my spirit, clothed immortal,
Wings its flight to realms of day
This my song through endless ages
Jesus led me all the way.
This my song through endless ages
Jesus led me all the way.

My, how these hymns bring back memories. Memories belong to the past and new ones are made with the future. Hymns were sung consistently in churches until the mid 70's during the folk music era when a new group of music composers introduced a new kind of Christian music – contemporary Christian music. The church was losing its pull on the community especially among the young. Therefore, to bring the young population back into the church, modern day choruses were introduced. Traditional and electric guitars, and drums were brought into the music worship adding a whole new dimension to our music.

Hymns were being replaced by contemporary tunes such as *Our God is an Awesome God* and *Yesterday He Died for Me, Shine Jesus Shine* and *Lord I Lift Your Name on High.* Some of the music from the ministry of Keith and Melody Green such as *There is a Redeemer, How Majestic is Thy Name,* and *You are the One* were also popular for a time. Here are some examples of these contemporary choruses:

He is Lord

He is Lord, He is Lord.
He is risen from the dead
And He is Lord.
Ev'ry knee shall bow,
Ev'ry tongue confess
That Jesus Christ is Lord.

God is so Good

God is so good,
God is so good;
God is so good,
He's so good to me!

Today churches are searching for a balance between the older people and the younger people, bringing back the hymns but sometimes rewriting the words, to make them more in line with the way we talk today, dropping the 'thee's' and 'thou's'. At the same time music leaders are sticking with the current modern choruses mixing them in with an old hymn here and there. Regardless of the intergenerational music, there is one thing that is true within the Christ believing church, the music may change from one generation to the next but the inspired Word of God and the time tested theology will never change. This is the one thing that Maria Wiens found to be constant in her life.

Chapter 16

The Wiens' Life During the "turbulent, free lovin' sixties"

With the dawning of the sixties, new conveniences such as frost-free refrigerators, automatic washing machines, electric ranges, TV dinners, jell-o, cheese spread, and Wonder Bread became a way of life. It was also an era marked by protests, social changes, Medicare, The Quebec uprising, the space age and Vietnam. Baby boomers were becoming teenagers and young adults were entering college. Voting age in Canada is 21. In America they were also old enough to be drafted to war at eighteen, but not old enough to vote. This was a time when the young people tested the limits, looking to see what there was to be seen and changing the world forever by touching off a decade of experimentation.

The Sixties were also a personal time of sadness and happiness for Maria and her family. Whether we live to be 30 or 53 or even 100, every life comes to an end at some time but never when we plan for it to be convenient and certainly never without leaving an effect. The Bible tells us that there is a "right time to be born and the right time to die. A time to plant and a time reap. A time to cry and a time to laugh, a time to embrace and time to part, a time to hold and a time to let go, a time to search and a time to count your losses." (Ecclesiastes 3) Certainly in the 53 years that God allotted to Peter Peter Wiens, he did all of these things. In the fall of 1960, Peter and Maria had no more little ones at home during the day for the first time in 26 years. They sent Blondina, their last child, on the school bus along with the rest of the children. It must have been strange for Maria to have no one at home and very quiet too. To help with the operation of the farm, Peter and Maria had one of the older children stay at home for a year. Ed graduated from high school in the spring of 1960 and stayed on the farm for two years before moving on. This trend of having the oldest child stay at home started with Anna and ended with Beth. Lily also came home for one year when Maria needed her. In the summer of 1961, the family began to spill over into two other Provinces. Rose left Saskatchewan and started nurses training in Vancouver, B.C., while Herb was teaching and Lily was studying nursing in Winnipeg, Manitoba. Anna, Reuben, Ed, and Vi had completed their school years in Glenbush and were either helping at home or in Bible school.

Monday, September 25, 1961 started out like any other day. The children were roused out of their beds, ate breakfast, and were sent out the door to school. Peter Wiens, John Isaac, and his son Walter had purchased the Medstead railroad water tower with the plans of disassembling it. Peter planned to use his share to build an animal shelter in the same place where the burned down chicken barn had stood.

On that particular day, Peter and his son Ed, John Issac, and his sons Walter and David were at the job site. They had reached the point in their work where they were at the final corner of the foundation. This foundation was so well built that a bulldozer could not move it. Because of this challenge, coupled with the fact that they had a deadline to meet with railroad, they decided to try dynamite. Toward the end of the day, around 4 in the afternoon, they were dynamiting the last corner of the foundation when something went wrong. The dynamite did not go off, as it should have. Given this, they did not know if it had been lit, so Peter and Walter went to check it out. It had been a windy kind of day with the usual sprinkling of rain, and the wind kept blowing out the match to light the fuse. Finally, Walter suggested that perhaps the embers from a fire might help to light the fuse. No sooner than Walter had come back to where Peter was bent over the dynamite then the fuse went off, blowing Peter into the air.

Peter was instantly killed and in the presence of his Lord. Walter, who was standing within touching distance of Peter, was seriously hurt when the sand blasted into his eyes. Ed and David were standing about 20 feet from them. To this day, it is miracle that Walter survived that accident and didn't go blind. At the time of this accident, Walter's wife was pregnant with their first child. While one person's life was spared, another was taken. This day was a day that would forever be remembered in the Wiens family. The Wiens children had a father in the morning but were fatherless at the end of the day. Someday, in God's good time, the reason why things went the way they did will be revealed to their children.

Ordinarily names of people injured or killed in an accident are not released without first notifying the next of kin. The events of that day were handled rather poorly by the news media. Jeremiah 29:11 tells us "God has plans to prosper us rather than harm us as well as a future and a hope". In thinking about this day from an adult point of view, I marvel at how Maria was initially protected from hearing of the accident. One of the routines that Maria followed each day was to listen to the 5:00 o'clock evening news on the radio. That particular day, when she went to turn the radio on, she heard a voice that specifically told her not to. A little later on she went towards the radio again – again the voice told her not to turn it on. When Ed came home around 8:00 that night, she knew that something had happened. She asked Ed where Dad was. Whatever he told her is not known and she never really told anyone. Had she turned the radio on in spite of that 'voice', she would have heard about the death of her husband on the radio. She was also protected from harm that day in that she did not own a telephone. If she would have had one, her relatives and others might have tried to call her.

Shortly after that Abe Pauls, the church pastor, came to talk to her. He helped her make the necessary arrangements and notifications to the children. How hard that must have been to let her children know that their dad was gone.

I think Peter had a premonition that summer that something might happen to him because he asked Rose, who had moved the furthest away, if she would come to his funeral. There is a character in the Bible named Job who went through much travail and difficulty. He lost all of his sons and daughters, his health, and his fortune. The Bible tells us that when these things happened, he never blamed God for these losses. But it tells us that Job said, "The Lord gave and the Lord has taken away; may the name of the Lord be praised." (Job 2:21b). Where was Maria's "hope and a future" that day? It was in the same place that it had been when the chicken barn burned down in 1944 and during the depression in the 30's. Her hope was firmly anchored in God. As she told someone later, she didn't know why Peter had to die that day but she was sure it was for his 'good'. Needless to say, his passing left a big void in his family, a void no one would ever be able to fill, and he was sorely missed by all who knew him. To the very end of his life he remained faithful to God, his family, and his church and he had gained the respect and love of his community.

On the Sunday morning of the funeral, the family spent some time singing together. They recorded some songs that went onto a record that also contained a solo Peter had sung at his mother-in-law's 90th birthday celebration earlier that summer. The second solo was the song he sung at the double wedding of his nieces in 1956. What a special treat it is to have on tape the sound of the voice of the loved ones. One of the pieces chosen was a poem which Rueben read as a reminder to Maria that despite everything, God was still in control.

He Maketh No Mistake (Author Unknown)

My Father's way may twist and turn,
My heart may throb and ache,
But in my soul I'm glad to know,
He maketh no mistake.

My cherished plans may go astray,
My hopes may fade away,
But I'll trust my Lord to lead
For He doth know the way.

Tho' night be dark, and it may seem
That day will never break,
I'll pin my faith, my all in Him,
He maketh no mistake.

For by and by the mist will lift
And plain it all He'll make,
Through all the way, tho' dark to me
He made not one mistake.

In 2003, around Easter time, our choir sang a song written by Jeff Joyner, our worship leader. The title of it was "*I Will Rest in You*". He has given me permission to use these words. When I first heard it, it reminded me immediately Maria's faith and the source of her strength.

I will rest in You
I will rest in You my God
I will rest in You

Waiting for You patiently

I am anchored in Your love
I will rest in You
I will rest in You

©2002 Jeff Joyner, JT Music

How Maria hurt during that time. There was one absolute reliable Anchor she could hold onto in her loneliness and pain. This was the established trust she had in the Lord. He knew what He was doing and it was in the best interests of all concerned. She still had seven between the ages of six and sixteen children at home. It was a difficult task to raise children, especially when they become teenagers. Now that task was thrust upon her brave shoulders, and hers alone, without the help of a husband. Yet during that entire time she was able, for the most part, to keep control of her tongue and temper and stay the course when the load became harder and harder.

Solomon said that there was a time to be sad and a time to put away sadness. July 7, 1962 opened another chapter in the family history. Maria and Lily traveled by Greyhound bus to Vineland, Ontario to attend the wedding of her oldest son, Herbert Peter Wiens, to Viola Patsy Willms whom he had met in Bible school. The newlyweds drove to Glenbush where the rest of the family met the newest member of the family before settling in Winnipeg where Herb taught high school. Between 1962 and the end of 1967, four other children were united in marriage. Rose Hildegard married Ernst Penner on September 11, 1964. Lily Florence was united with Lawrence Irvin Willems, a farmer from Waldheim, on June 17, 1966. The weddings of Rose and Lily were the only two Wiens weddings held in the Glenbush M.B. church. On August 26, 1967 Elizabeth Helen married Ernest Frank Friesen in Saskatoon. At the end of the year, Edward Peter married Marjorie Marie Wiens in Abbotsford, B.C.

The 60's also brought new precious little lives into the family, making Maria a grandmother. The first grandchild, Howard Keith, was born on December 28 of 1965 to Herb and Vi Wiens in Vancouver, B.C., where Herb was involved in selling life insurance. Tamara Cheryl Penner, daughter of Rose and Ernie Penner, entered the world on May 12 of 1966. When Tamara was about 6 weeks old, Rose and Ernie, together with Herb and Vi, traveled to Glenbush to attend the wedding of their oldest sister, Lily, and introduce the little ones to their grandmother. On March 31 of 1968 a second grandson, Dana Andrew Penner, made her a grandma three times over. One and a half years later, Herb and Vi adopted Geraldine (Gerry) Jennifer Wiens, who was born on June 7 of 1968.

Maria stayed on the farm until the end of June 1966 and sold it in 1967. During the five year period prior, she rented out parts of it and /or farmed it with the help of Reuben, who had rented two quarters of his own close by. Her reasons for moving into Saskatoon were really twofold. Firstly, she did not know how to drive and realized how isolated she was. In the event of an emergency, she did not even have a telephone on the farm. Second, none of the remaining sons showed an interest in farming and wanted to pursue other ventures. With four children still in school, she made the decision to leave the farm and bought a four-bedroom house in Saskatoon, Sk. at 1110 Ave J North. The Mennonite Brethren church the family attended was less than a block away. There her house once again became full. Melita and Blondina were in grade school, Naomi and George were in high school, and Reuben, Anna, and Vi were attending the University of Saskatchewan. City life not only had more to offer in the way of conveniences, but also more temptations that the family had not been privy to before.

It was here that the family experienced the presence of their first television and telephone – items that quickly became a way of life for the family. Maria was close to her family. Her mother, two sisters Agnes and Elizabeth, and in-laws (Peter's sister and her husband) Justina and Cornelius Siemens all lived not far away. For the first time she could walk over and visit them whenever time allowed her to do so. We could always tell when she was talking to one of them on the phone because it would be in German. What's more, we could always tell when she was talking about us even though we never understood a single word she said because she dropped names in her conversation.

The summer that Maria moved from Glenbush, six other families from the Glenbush Mennonite Brethren church also moved away. Glenbush experienced other changes as well. Once again the Glenbush High School underwent a change. Due to finances and practicality, it was consolidated with the next largest school in Medstead four miles away. Today the grade school is also consolidated with the Medstead School. What was once a school is now the Heritage Center in Glenbush with exhibits remembering the 'good ole days'.

Maria also got her first job, at the University in the housekeeping department. She worked there for four years before she was laid off. Once, on her way to work, she fell on the icy street as she got off the bus and broke her arm. After her lay off, she started to work for one of her former employers cleaning her home. From that start, word of the quality of her work got around and she had enough work to keep her busy until she retired in 1976 at the age of 65. She never learned to drive, but depended on the local bus system, which was quite good in Saskatoon. Living in the city took some adjusting. For the first time, she needed to be concerned about the physical protection of the younger children. During her first summer, she had surgery. During this time she arranged for the newlyweds, Lily and Lawrence, to stay with the younger children. That August she took all of the younger children (with the exception of one) on their first trip out of the province to British Columbia. They traveled via the Greyhound Bus. George had a job at an ice cream store, so was not able to go. Her children grew up. The last two children graduated from high school in 1971 and 1972 respectively. In 1969 she had the chance of a lifetime to travel with tour group to the Holy Land. While there she almost drowned in the Dead Sea. This was her first of several trips overseas.

1969 brought another loss to Maria, that of her mother. After many years of living with one child or another, Maria's mother, Anna Pankratz Derksen, was moved to a nursing home where she spent the last few years of her life. When the Derksen family knew that the end of the 98-year-old Derksen matriarch's life was coming to an end, they hurried to the nursing home to bid their farewells to her. She breathed her last breath on October 13, 1969. They buried her in the Borden M.B. Cemetery where her husband and many of her children are also buried. Anna Derksen was the last member of the original Borden M.B. Church to die.

Anna and Gerhard Derksen

They were the parents of Maria Derksen. Grandpa Derksen died in 1933 – a year before Peter and Maria were married. Peter never met her father.

Anna Derksen was 90 years old when Peter died.

She died in 1969 at the age of 98. She never spoke English although it has been rumored that she understood some of it.

Justina Wiens was born in Russia on March 4, 1901. She married Kornelius Siemens in Russia on June 12, 1921. They came to Canada in 1926 with two children, Kornelius and Nellie. Settling first in southern Saskatchewan where they originally were farmers, they eventually moved to Saskatoon where he started a trucking company known as Siemens Transport. Two of their sons, Walter and Erwin followed him into the transport business.

Justina & Kornelius died on July 20, 1985 and October 14, 1966 respectively.

Sara Wiens was born on October 18, 1898 in Russia. She married her stepfather's brother, Nicolai P. Pauls (born December 22, 1892) on March 3, 1918. Together with their four children, they left Russia after Nicolai had to leave the country for his own safety.

They first went to Waldheim where they stayed for two years before moving on to Glenbush where they farmed.

Nicolai was the founding pastor, a position he held until they moved to British Columbia in 1956.
Nicolai died on October 30, 1976. Sara died on December 29, 1982.

Margareta was born in Russia on January 20, 1903.

She married Johann Enns (born June 24, 1896) on November 22, 1975 in Waldheim, Saskatchewan. At the time that the Wiens children left Russia, Margareta was already engaged to John

John and Margaret settled in the Glenbush area where they were farmers. They moved from Glenbush to Elm Creek,

Manitoba in 1948, eventually moving all the way to Ontario. John died on March 5, 1980. Margaret outlived him by six years passing away on March 24, 1986.

Katarina (Tina) Pauls was born to Maria Eck Wiens Pauls on December 14, 1912 in Russia. She married Peter Warkentin (born November 7, 1906) on December 28, 1946. After the disappearance of her father in 1937, she and her sister took care of their mother. Peter died on March 9, 1972 in Russia.

Tina eventually immigrated to Germany and died 20 years later on October 26, 1992. Peter and Tina had three children of which Lena, the oldest child, corresponds with members of the extended Wiens family.

Peter's youngest half sister, Njessa & her husband
Boris Schmidt and their family.

Njessa &Boris Schmidt
with some of their
children and
grandchildren
in 1991

Njessa Pauls was born on February 18, 1921 to Maria and Peter Pauls.
Peter never saw his parents or half sisters again after he and his sisters left Russia.
Soviet Union borders were closed before that part of his family could escape.

She married Bernhard (Boris) Schmidt (born February 25, 1920) on April 30, 1949 in
Russia. Boris was a lay preacher and spent several years in prison for his faith. Boris
passed away on March 12, 2004 at the age of 84.

Today, with the exception of Njessa, all of Peter's family is in eternity where they are
forever together after so many years. Njessa is in her 80's and is still living in Russia
with two of her daughters.

Anna Derksen, the 90 year old Mother-in-law of Peter Wiens

She died in 1969 at the age of 98

Peter with his six daughters in 1951
Back Row: Rose, Lily, Peter Wiens
Middle row: Vi, Anna holding Naomi,
Front row: Beth

1951 family picture in front of the '49 blue 2 door Ford
This was the only brand new car he ever owned.

Peter with his six sons in 1951.
Back Row L to R: Herb, Peter;
Third row: Reuben, Ed;
Second Row: Vic and John
Front Row: George

The Wiens family in the summer of 1951.
The boys are to the left while the girls are on the right.

A family picture around 1959.
1st row: Naomi, Melita & Blondina
2nd: Beth, John, Vic and George
3rd: Rose, Anna, Lily, and Vi
4th: Ed, Herb and Reuben

Notice the lattice fence that Lily helped Dad build!

Peter and Maria on
Their Silver Anniversary in
1959
Front Row: Naomi, Mom,
Blondina, Dad and Melita
Second Row: Anna, Beth,
John, Vic, and George
Lily, Reuben, Herb, Ed,
Rose and Vi
This was the last family
picture to be taken while
Peter was alive.
Peter died 2 years later.

The first family wedding
Herb & Vi Wiens
July 7, 1962

The Wiens family in December 1967 taken on the day before
the wedding of Ed & Marge Wiens.

This was the last family picture taken where everyone was in one place.
Back row L to R: George, Naomi, Vi, Melita, Anna and John.
Middle row: Reuben, Herb, Lawrence & Lily Willems, Ed & Marge Wiens, Ernie
Penner and Vic.
Front row: Beth & Ernie Friesen, Viola Wiens (Herb's wife), Howard Wiens (2
years old), Maria, Tamara (1 ½ years old), Rose Penner, Blondina

Chapter 17

New Frontiers

The 70's and 80's saw many changes in the Wiens household. The last two children graduated from high school, nine more children married, and 23 more grandchildren made their way into the world. In the fall of 1972, after Blondina graduated from High School, Maria lived by herself for the first time in her life.

There were also more family weddings. George Peter Wiens married Edith Lorraine Neumann on October 1 of 1970. The weddings of two daughters occurred in the summer of 1972. Violet Viola married an Englishman, John Howard Parris from Calgary, on July 8 of 1872. Naomi Ruth married an American, Phillip James Kapplehoff, on August 25 of 1972. Reuben Peter Wiens married Sharon Dale Sibley on August 17 of 1974. Victor Peter Wiens married Pollyanna Beatty on March 29 of 1975. They were married for a number of years before their marriage ultimately ended in divorce. Anna Grace Wiens married Kenneth Peter Kroeker, a farmer from Waldheim Sk, on July 19 of 1975.

The biggest change for Maria was not so much her retirement but the fact that she remarried. She referred to this event as a turning point in her life. In 1976 God brought back into her life another companion. That summer she became reacquainted with someone she had known all of her life, a kind and gentle man named Abram William Martens. The courtship was so unsuspected that the first time they sat in church together was on the day they announced their engagement. Maria's sister Ella was heard to say in German to her husband, Isaac, "What, could this be Our Maria?" Their fall engagement announcement was a total surprise to those who knew them. I will let her words describe it as she wrote them in a letter to Dina:

> *"Now you better lie down when you read on for you might be shocked. Here goes - can you believe that my age dropped about 40 years? You better believe it, I'm doing the same thing you are doing, oh no not quite, we still are more reserved, but we enjoy each other's company. It's funny what it does to a person if a man has an interest in you. If marriage is to follow, which might but now we both are not ready to make that decision although we have known each other all our lives. Would you be against it if I should marry again or would you think it foolish if me? Nobody knows about us here in Saskatoon unless the neighbors, Willems saw us when he picked me up on Saturday. The evening was so beautiful so he decided to take me out for a long ride. Can you guess who my friend is? You are the only one that would know him."*

Even Dina didn't know for several weeks after her return who the 'mystery man' was until someone told her. Maria was a changed woman then; although she had always been happy, she was very happy and excited. In October they announced their engagement to the total surprise of everyone and in November she retired from working as a housecleaner.

With all their family surrounding them, they celebrated the union of their marriage on the evening of December 30, 1976. All of Maria's children and grandchildren filled the entire choir loft of the church and watched her tie the knot with Abe Martens. How many children live to see their Mother get married? What a joyous occasion that was to see Maria, our Mother, after 15 years of widowhood, married again.

Following a month long honeymoon in Arizona, where one Abram's sisters lived, they returned to the cold northern country of Canada and set about building a brand new house - a house that was neither his nor hers but theirs. It was big enough to entertain the growing family, which now included not only her children and their families but his children and grandchildren as well.

I heard an account from one of my sisters who shed some more light on this very covert courting. Some months before the courting process had started, she had a dream where she was sitting on a concrete fence with our father, Peter Wiens, when Maria strolled by with a tall, handsome, white haired man. Peter told her that it was all right for her to do this. In the spring of 1976, she and her husband were in Saskatoon visiting Maria. They teased Maria, saying that she should get herself a Santa for Christmas. Later this same sister said, "I had a dream about you" and left it at that. In June after Blondina had left to live in Jasper for the summer months, Maria asked this sister, "What was your dream?" She responded by saying, "Why? Are you seeing someone?" Maria acknowledged that she was and told her who the 'mystery man' was. It was the man in her dream.

Allow me to introduce you to Abram William Martens, the second husband of Maria Wiens, and the only grandfather the grandchildren had on the Wiens side of things. Born on March 1 of 1902, Abe moved with his parents and seven brothers and sisters from Mountain Lake, Minnesota to Borden, Sask. in October of 1912. After the sudden death of his mother on July 1 of 1916, his father remarried. Five girls were born this second marriage. After living in a homestead in the Hoffnungfeld School area for a year, they moved to another homestead where they lived for five years. After his marriage to Sara Nickels, they made their first home in the Diefenbaker shack. Abe and Sara had four children-Ruby, Les, Joyce, and Harvey. Sara died on July 20 of 1971. After five and a half years of batching, Abe married Maria. Prior to his retirement, Abe worked as grain buyer and lived in Saskatoon for a few years before moving back to Borden. There he was a farmer until 1958 when he again moved to Saskatoon – this time for good.

Abe and Maria's retirement years were not spent in the rocking chair on the front porch. I once asked her what she did with all the time that she had on her hands. Her reply was that she was busier than she was before her retirement.

Their early retirement years were spent bowling with a group of seniors, fishing in the summers, and traveling around to visit the children. Maria together with another lady also continued to bring joy to the hearts of old folks at the Personal Care Home by playing the piano for them. She also volunteered her time by accompanying people to their doctor appointments and other places.

Three more family weddings took place after their marriage. Her youngest daughter, Blondina Johanna, married Russell Richard Funk on August 27 of 1977. This marriage came after Maria and Russ's grandmothers played the roles of matchmakers. They introduced the two young ones to each other and the rest became history. Melita Margaret married Timothy Anthony Kudel the following year on June 17 of 1978. Two marriages occurred in 1982, John Peter Wiens married Marjorie Joy Gorman on September 11 of 1982 and Ed married Donna Lynne Beaton on September 14 of 1982. (This was several years after Ed's first marriage ended in divorce).

Dwight Eisenhower once said that there was no tragedy in life like the death of a child. During the early years of Abe and Maria's marriage, each lost an adult child to death. On July 4 of 1979, Maria's world was rocked again when she got a call informing her that her youngest son, George, had been electrocuted while performing his duties as a concrete pump operator. During the early years of their marriage, Abe's oldest daughter also died on Easter Sunday from cancer. And so in these times of sadness, they comforted each other.

Abe was a kind and gentle man. He was a man who kept his promise. Prior to his marriage, he promised to be kind and good to Maria. The grandkids loved him. He accepted Maria's children as if they were his own. How we appreciated that. Abe always had a kind word for everyone. Church was an important factor in his life. One church service in particular stood out in Abe's memory. One summer when we went to Saskatchewan, he told us that the Sunday before the pastor of the church had preached on a subject that was rarely ever talked about. He had fashioned his sermon around the subject of hell. After sharing his thoughts on the previous week's message, he expressed that he was so grateful that really true believers knew for a fact that they would someday go to heaven. Heaven was a place of peace, love, and joy while hell was just the opposite.

One of the highlights of the 90's was Maria's surprise 80th birthday. What started out as a limo ride to go out for coffee with her daughter Rose and granddaughter Tamara, ended up as a big surprise party at Tim and Melita's home where all of her children, with the exception of Ed and Herb, waited for her. She later wrote that she felt like a queen and feasted on that day of happiness for over a year. Together her children, some of their mates, and the grandchildren, were able to give back just a little of what she had spent 80 years giving to others.

During the 90's she was able to attend the weddings of six of her grandchildren and became a great grandmother 16 times over. She met most of the great grandchildren who were born during that time. Her first great grandchild, Brandon James Wiens, was born on August 13 of 1991.

Approximately ten years after their marriage, Abe started showing signs of Alzheimer's. Alzheimer's affects the part of the brain that controls thought, memory and language. He started showing signs of mild forgetfulness, and by 1990 he could not remember what day it was or familiar faces such as Maria. Yet he could remember such events as the death of his mother like it was yesterday, even though she had died more than 60 years ago. During those years, Maria protected him in the best way she could by pinning a piece of paper to his jacket stating his name, address, and phone number in case he got lost when he went out to get his coffee. Eventually Maria's health would no longer permit her to take care of her husband and she found it necessary to place him in a nursing home where he spent his last three years.

In April of 1999, Maria sold the home they had built together and moved into a retirement home at the Lutheran Towers in Saskatoon. A few days after she moved, she experienced the loss of her second husband of 22 years. In the morning hours of April 19 of1999, Abe went home to meet the Lord that he loved so much. He was 95 years old. Their years together were years of love, joy, travel, and looking after the interests of each other.

The Bible tells us in heaven there will be no more death, crying, or pain. In fact he will wipe every tear from their eyes. I can't begin to imagine what that will be like. One thing I do know is that there not any of the things we experience here such as disease, disability, or even aging. It's a whole new world where believers see Jesus face to face rather than through a veil. Maria had a song that was a favorite of hers that she wanted sung at her memorial entitled "*The Home over There*"by D. W. C. Huntington. The words of the song go like this:

1. *O think of the home over there*
By the side of the river of life,
Where the saints, all immortal and fair,
Are robed in their garments of white.

2. *Over there, over there,*
O think of the home over there,
Over there, over there,
O think of the home over there.

3. *O think of the friends over there*
Who before us the journey have trod,
Of the songs that they breathe on the air
In their home in the palace of God.

4. *Over there, over there,*
O think of the friends over there,
Over there, over there
O think of the friends over there.

5. *My Saviour is now over there,*
There my kindred and friends are at rest,
Then away from my sorrow and care
Let me fly to the land of the blest.

6. Over there, over there
My Saviour is now over there
Over there, over there
My Saviour is now over there.

7. I'll soon be at home over there,
For the end of my journey I see;
Many dear to my hear, over there
Are watching and waiting for me.

8. Over there, over there
I'll soon be at home over there
Over there, over there
I'll soon be at home over there.

After the death of her husband, Maria didn't feel well physically. A checkup at the doctor indicated that she had developed an aortic aneurysm. An aneurysm is a bulge that forms on the wall of a blood vessel. It becomes dangerous when this bulge moves or bursts. Although this aneurysm was operable, she chose not to go through this process. Years earlier, she had developed heart problems and thought that she might not survive the surgery. During the nineteen months allotted her, she continued to live for God. In the retirement home she played the piano for the Sunday night sing along right up to the Sunday she entered the hospital for the last time.

On October 6 of 1999, she experienced yet another sudden loss – that of her six month old great grandchild Sadie Lynn Wiggins from SIDS (Sudden Infant Death Syndrome) in Calgary, Alberta. She traveled to Calgary to comfort Heather and Dean in their loss. Here she exemplified one of her most endearing characteristics by putting Heather's needs ahead of her own. During this time, Maria was calm and knew WHOM she belonged to and that He held her in the palm of HIS hand. The knowledge that she had what she referred to as a 'ticking time bomb' in her body was a gift to her children. It was an opportunity for them to say to her what needed to be said. I recall a conversation I had with her one day. It had been a particularly frustrating week where nothing went right. I asked her if she had ever experienced a time in her life when she realized that the more she knew – the less she knew. She affirmed to me that this was indeed true many times in her life. She was a comfort and encouragement to many people including me.

Because all of the children who lived close by were out of town, she spent her 89th birthday with her grandchildren and great grandchildren. They made this day very special for her.

She had always had an interest in what was going on in the world around her. United States had a Presidential election on November 4 of 2000, which turned out to be a very unusual election as elections go. Republican George W. Bush was running against Democrat Al Gore. Due to unprecedented problems with the ballots and counting the votes, the election results were not announced until three months later. Maria watched all of this news with great interest and amusement and made the comment that she wondered whom they were talking to because she certainly could understand how the ballots worked and she was 89 years old. She never did find out the results of that election. On November 12, 2000, she called the senior home coordinator to let him know she would not be able to come in that evening to play piano for the sing along and she checked into the hospital for the last time. She passed away on November 17 of 2000.

In thinking about the life of Maria, I recall a conversation I heard about that was important in the scheme of things. When Maria was in her 60's, Beth asked her how she viewed life as she got closer to eternity. The picture that Maria painted was kind of a Thomas Kincaid picture. Thomas Kincaid is an artist who earned the reputation as the 'Painter of Lights'. His pictures rarely include people, but contain bridges, towns, snow scenes, vintage cars, horse drawn carriages, and houses – well lit homes. The streets of his paintings are well traveled. A light in the window of a home will always attract the eye of an observer on the street as a warm and welcoming place, while a dark house seems cold and uninviting to a travel-worn person. Maria told Beth she viewed eternity as traveling in the country in the dark and seeing a house in the distance with its lights on. The lights meant that there was warmth and a presence of people under its roof.

Maria has finished her life journey and has entered the door of that house with countless other family members. It is now up to us finish our journey in a manner that is consistent with the standards she set for us so that someday we too will go through the door of that House with its lights beckoning us home.

"Hitherto hath the Lord helped us."

1 Samuel 7:12

We cordially invite you to share

with us the Lord's blessing

at our wedding

on Thursday, the thirtieth of December

nineteen hundred and seventy-six

at two p.m.

Central M.B. Church

32nd Street and Avenue I

Saskatoon, Saskatchewan

Abram W. Martens

and

Maria Wiens

FOLLOWING THE PROGRAM
FRIENDSHIP TEA WILL BE SERVED
IN THE LOWER AUDITORIUM
NO GIFTS, PLEASE   R.S.V.P.

Abe and Maria Martens

Their Wedding Day - December 30, 1976

Maria and Abe with some of the grandchildren on her birthday
Grandchildren: Barb, Iris, Heather and Jan

The family had a surprise birthday
Party for Maria on
Her 80th birthday
On November 4, 1990

All the daughters and 3 of the 5 sons were
present along with some of the spouses and
grandchildren.

Maria and her boys
Back row: Reuben, Vic and John
Front row: Abe and Maria Martens

Maria & Abe together with the spouses:

Back row: Lawrence Willems, John Parris,
Tim Kudel, Russ Funk, Ken Kroeker
Front Row: Marjorie (John) Wiens,
parents, Sharon (Reuben) Wiens

November 4, 1990

Maria
doing what she did best – bringing the joy of
music to the hearts of many.

Three generations of women

Rose Penner, Maria and Rose's
daughter, Tamara Penner.

Tamara announced her engagement
at this party.

Maria & Abe with all her daughters

Back Row L to R:
Melita Kudel, Beth Friesen, Rose Penner, Anna Kroeker, Naomi Kapplehoff
Front: Blondina Funk, Lily Willems, Abe, Maria, and Vi Parris

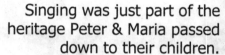

Singing was just part of the heritage Peter & Maria passed down to their children.

Naomi with her Mother on her 80th birthday.

They are 40 years apart on this day.

PART 2

REMEMBRANCES

FAMILY TRIBUTES

From Maria's 80th Birthday

November 2, 1990

*"Let yourself be cradled in the arms of those who
love you. We are never too old to be held."*
- Jane Latus Emmert

The Grandchildren Remember

The house Abe and Maria built on Ave G had quite a good-sized backyard. One of the things Maria liked to do was gardening. More importantly, Maria was a grandma to over thirty grandchildren and many great grandchildren. She loved them all and they loved her.

When the grandkids were still very young, she started to crochet afghans for each of them to be given to them when they married. No two were alike. By the time she was no longer able to knit, she had her closet full. When she sold her home in 1999, she gave these blankets to the grandchildren who were not yet married as well as to her own children. Today that pink crocheted blanket is on the end of my guest bed as a reminder of my mother.

Maria loved Christmas!! Each year, she sent out Christmas cards to each person in the family which included a handwritten verse she liked. She usually had family dinners in the basement of her home where it nice and cool in the summer and warm and cozy in the winter. At the end of the long eating area was a tree that was decked with the usual ornaments but tucked in the lower branches among the ornaments were little matchbox cars tied up with string just in eye range of the little grandkids. She would never get the kids any kind of toys such as guns that represented violence.

After the dinner and the cleanup, music and the opening of gifts would follow. Christmas was special in her home. It was one of the most important days of the year – it was the day that she celebrated the birth of the Christ child who came into the world to save us from our sins. That's what Christmas was about.

Rather than try to put into words what the various grandchildren thought of her, I am going to use their own testimonials but before we do that, let me introduce each of the grandchildren to you along with what they are doing today.

Some of the grandchildren lived in close proximity to her home and therefore had more encounters with their grandparents. Others, on the other hand, were spread out all over the continent – from Ottawa in the east to Vancouver on the west and points beyond south stretching as far away as Florida. Their encounters were few and far between with communications being limited to telephone or mail.

1. ***Lily Florence Wiens*** married Lawrence Willems, (born June 25, 1931) a farmer from Waldheim on June 17, 1966. Today both Lily and Lawrence are retired and live in Waldheim. They have two daughters – Iris Valerie on May 22, 1972. Iris is an electrical engineer in Ottawa, Ontario.

Heather Angela was born on February 3, 1974. She married Dean Wiggins (born July 1, 1960) on November 6, 1994. They are the parents of three sons – Kain Michael on March 22, 1995; Caydon Rence on August 15, 2000 and Kellon Aston on May 7, 2002; and one daughter Sadie Lyn born on April 7, 1999. Sadly Sadie died at six months of age from SIDS. Today Heather is a single parent raising the three boys in Hinton, Alberta.

*2. **Herb Peter Wiens*** married Viola Willms (born March 16, 1939) on July 7, 1962. They had two children – one son, Howard Keith born on December 28, 1965 and one adopted daughter, Geraldine (Gerry) Jennifer born on June 7, 1968. Herb & Vi subsequently divorced. Herb is now retired and living in New Westminster, B.C.

Today **Howard** is an attorney in Abbotsford, B.C. He married Cheri Lynn Weinhauer (born Oct. 6, 1964) on August 24, 1990 in Burnaby, B.C. They are the parents of three children – Jodie Corine on September 27, 1993; Camden Keith on October 25, 1996 and Brenna Arlene on September 20, 1998.

Gerry is a single mother of one son, Brandon James Wiens on August 13, 1991 and one daughter, Katerina May Wiens on October 29, 1999. She lives in the Vancouver area.

*3. **Rose Hildegard Wiens*** married Ernst Penner (born May 19, 1934) on September 11, 1964. Today Rose and Ernie are retired and getting ready to relocate from their home in Survey, B.C. to Vernon, B.C. where they are building a house. Rose and Ernie have two children – Tamara Cheryl born on May 12, 1966 and Dana Andrew on March 31, 1968.

Tamara married Paul David Goodwin (born Oct. 31, 1960) on March 28, 1992. They have two sons – Matthew Joseph on October 14, 1994 in San Francisco, Ca.; Spencer William on May 2, 1996 in Fort Lauderdale, Florida and one daughter – Kathrina Mae on September 18, 2000 also in Florida. Today Tamara and her family live in Woodinville, Wa.

Dana married Robyn Louise Bowell (born Aug. 5, 1968) on March 26, 1994. They moved from Canada to the Caribbean where he studied medicine and then to England. They now reside in Williamsville, New York. They are the parents of four children – one son, Luke Peter Connor on August 11, 1996; three daughters - Savannah Grace on October 5, 1998; Micah Rose Sharon on June 30, 2000 and Lauryn Faith on May 8, 2002. All of Dana's children were born in Canada with the exception of Lauryn who was born in England.

*4. **Anna Grace Wiens*** married Kenneth Peter Kroeker, (Oct. 29, 1930) a farmer from Waldheim, Sk. They are still farming in the area and have two daughters and one son. Their twin daughters, Janet Kimberly and Barbara Anne were born on September 1, 1976.

Janet is married Lorn Jeremy Gieck, (born June 21, 1976) a music pastor in Saskatoon on October 24, 1998. They have one daughter, Judith Charis born on December 23, 2002 and a wee son, Theodore Spencer born July 4, 2004.

Their second daughter, **Barbara** married Kimberly (Kim) Wayne Worthington (born August 30, 1974) on July 13, 2002. Kim is currently a student at Bethany Bible College and Barb is involved in ministry with Youth for Christ in Saskatoon.

Robert Peter Kroeker was born two years later on August 14, 1978. He is living in Calgary, Alberta. Rob married Patricia Marie Reynolds (born December 13, 1974) on March 15, 2003. He is a stepfather to Pat's daughter, Richelle.

5. **_Reuben Peter Wiens_** married Sharon Dale Sibley (born October 11, 1948) on August 17, 1974. They also have two sons – **Travis** Kent on January 21, 1979 and **Darren** Kirk on December 5, 1981. Travis is working on his PHD at the University of Saskatchewan in Saskatoon. Darren is a student at Simon Fraser University hoping to graduate in the spring of 2005. He also has plans to pursue his master's degree next year.

6. After the divorce of his first marriage, **_Edward Peter Wiens_** married Donna Lynne Beaton (August 28, 1953) on September 14, 1982. They have one daughter, **Emily** Alison born on July 20, 1983. Ed & Donna live in Toronto where Ed is a professional musician. Emily is currently a second year student at the University of Waterloo.

7. **_Violet Viola Wiens_** married an Englishman, John Howard Parris (born August 6, 1947) from Calgary on July 8, 1972. While Vi is a retired teacher, John continues to teach. They have two sons– Justin Francis was born August 17, 1975 in Kitimat, B.C.

Justin married Rachel Deanna Filby (born Jan. 7, 1981) on October 5, 2002. Justin and Rachel are living in Calgary where Justin works and Rachel is a drama student.

Jonathan Peter Parris was born on June 11, 1978 in Jasper B. C. Today Jonathan is working in Whistler, B.C.

8. **_Elizabeth Helen (Beth) Wiens_** married Ernest Frank Friesen (Jan. 1, 1945) on August 26, 1967 in Saskatoon. Beth and Ernie are the parents of two sons – Jason Harrow on September 19, 1971; Trevor Julian on October 11, 1973 and one daughter Erin Maria Leann on April 8, 1979. Beth and her family live in Woodinville, Wa.

Jason married Jennifer Dawn Smith Jessup (born August 29, 1974) on August 29, 1994. They are the parents of two one son – Caden Jacob Riker on August 29, 2002 and one daughter – Laine Arwen Elizabeth on October 23, 2003. They live in Pittsburg, PA where Jason is doing his residency in medicine.

Trevor married Jaime Nicole Powers (born February 6, 1977) on November 9, 2001 in Hawaii. They are living in Sammamish, Wa.

Erin is currently living in Los Angeles, CA where she is working and going to school.

9. **_John Peter Wiens_** married Marjorie Joy Gorman (born May 24, 1953) on September 11, 1982. They currently live in Vernon, B.C. and have one daughter, FMichaela Joy Gorman Wiens born on August 23, 1984. **Michaela** has completed two years of university and is currently living in Vancouver. **Peter** James Gorman Wiens was born on July 23, 1987. Peter is still living at home and is a student in high school.

10. **_Victor Peter Wiens_** married Pollyanna Beatty on March 29, 1975. They were married for a number of years before their marriage ended in divorce. He married Deanna Merrill on October 14, 1988. Although Vic never had any children of his own,

he is a stepfather to Deanna's children, Christopher Alan Merrill (born November 19, 1976) and Sara Rae Merrill (born August 3, 1977). Chris is living in Issaquah, Wa.

Sara married James Phillip Richie on June 27, 1998. They are the parents of two boys - Coleman James Alexander Richie born on December 17, 1998 and Mason Christopher Richie born June 29, 2000.

Victor married Elizabeth Jean Sanderson Burke (born Aug. 31, 1953) on November 22, 2003. Liz is an attorney while Vic is involved in construction. **Joseph** Ryan Burke was born on September 4, 1989 and **Stuart** Michael Burke born on August 11, 1994.

*11. **Gerhard (George) Peter Wiens*** married Edith Lorraine Neumann (born Oct. 10, 1970) on October 10, 1970. They brought two sons into the world: Ryan Kade on December 22, 1972 and Joel Lee on December 16, 1975. Both boys were born in Burnaby, B.C.

Two years after the death of George in 1979, **Edith** married Hal Toews (born Sept. 1, 1946) on April 15, 1981. Edith and Hal are living in Abbotsford, B.C. where Hal is a retired teacher and Edith is still working.

Ryan married Michelle Angela Cameron (born December 13, 1970) on October 6, 2001 and is the proud father of a young daughter, Mary Teresa (Tess) born on June 21, 2003. Ryan and Michelle are studying theology in Kitchener, Ontario.

Joel is a second year student at Queen's University in Kingston, Ontario where he is studying medicine.

*12. **Naomi Ruth Wiens*** married an American, Phillip James Kapplehoff (born February 1, 1949) on August 25, 1972. They are currently living in the Seattle area in Washington State. They have three children – two daughters and one son. Kendra Renee was born on October 22, 1974; Nadine Maria on November 14, 1976 and Rhome Gabriel on Janaury 21, 1979.

Kendra married John Everett Heffelfinger, (born July 4, 1973) a police officer in Flagstaff, Arizona on October 3, 1998 and has a five-year-old son, Ryan Everett born on October 18, 1999 and a two-year-old daughter, Reagan Elizabeth born on Valentines Day, February 14, 2002.

Nadine is serving in the United States Army; she was stationed in Korea for 15 months. Following her return from Korea, she was transferred to Fort Riley, Kansas and deployed to Iraq for four months. She is currently based at Fort Riley, Kansas.

Rhome is disabled and living in Bellingham under the care of O'Brien Resources.

*13. **Melita Margaret Wiens*** married Timothy Anthony Kudel (born July 30, 1952) on June 17, 1978. Today Tim and Melita live in the Edmonton, Alberta area. They have three children – two daughters Leah Marie born on January 18, 1984; Christina Lynn born on April 20, 1985 and Mark Alexander on August 27, 1987.

Leah is currently studying dance and drama as it relates to worship with YWAM in Norway.

Christina is a first year student at university in Saskatoon while **Mark** is still at home and in high school.

14. ***Blondina Johanna Wiens*** married Russell Richard Funk (born December 3, 1956) on August 27, 1977 in Saskatoon. Blondina and Russ are living in Mitchell, Manitoba. They have two sons- Matthew Lee born on August 27, 1983 and Mark Russell born on March 10, 1986.

Their oldest son, **Matthew Lee** married Denica Leigh McLean (born Oct. 25, 1983) on February 14, 2004 and lives in Steinbach, Manitoba. **Mark Russell** is a first year student at Briercrest Bible College in Caronport, Sk.

*** ***

Maria with her daughters in April 1999
Standing L to R: Blondina, Lily, Melita, Anna Naomi and Vi
Seated: Beth, Maria holding Sadie who was just a newborn, and Rose

Left:
Ed & Donna Wiens
September 14, 1982

Right:
Vic Wiens & Liz
Sanderson-Burke
2002

Gerry Wiens with her daughter Katerina;
Kendra Heffelfinger with her son Ryan - 2000

Happy Holidays!

Love,
The Wiggins

Heather Wiggins with sons, Kain (back), Caydon and Kellen (front) - 2003

Howard & Cheri Wiens
   With their children
      Camden, Brenna and Jodie
        - 2003

Jason and Jennifer Friesen
With Caden and Laine

Easter 2004

Justin and Rachel Parris
2002

Mark Kudel, Travis Wiens
& Brandon Wiens with Uncle
Reuben - 2000

Top Left: Michaela Wiens; Top Right: Russ & Dina Funk with
Matthew & Mark Funk

Ryan and Michelle Wiens with Tess

Tamara & Paul Goodwin
Kathrina, Spencer and Matthew
2004

Abe & Maria Martens with
Kendra, Nadine and Rhome

Kendra (top left), Iris, Grandma, Tamara
1990

Kapplehoff Family – 2004
Back row: Nadine, Rhome, Chip Heffelfinger
Middle: Phil, Naomi & Kendra Heffelfinger
Front: Ryan and Reagan Heffelfinger

Tricia & Rob Kroeker

Below: Jan & Lorn Gieck with their children (right) Judith & Theodore

Emily Wiens

Kristina, Leah & Mark Kudel - 2002

Sadie Wiggins - 1999(right)

Peter and Michaela Wiens - 2002

Grandsons at Maria's burial site
Left side: Robert Kroecker, Ryan Wiens
Right side: Joel Wiens and Justin Parris

Barb (Kroeker) & Kim Worthington
With Alexander Jamin Worthington
Summer - 2005

Jonathan Parris
2002

Trevor and Jamie Friesen - 2001

Erin Friesen - 2004

This was the last family picture taken of Maria on her 89th birthday. November 2, 2000

L to R: grandkids: Jan & Lorn Gieck, Maria, Kain Wiggins (Heather's son)
Back row: Barb Kroeker holding Caydon

Back row: Robyn and Dana
3rd row: Luke
2nd row: Micah Rose & Savannah
Front row: Lauryn

December 2003

Left: Rhome (2004)

Below: The grandchildren at Maria's
80th birthday in 1980

"I remember grandma as loving to play games – but no cheating!!! It was a 'no no' to even push the limits of a rule. She also loved pizza from Venice House. She was a little bit stern in my memory (probably because we didn't get whatever we wanted all the time) but I always knew she loved me. Grandma was quite a gardener – I especially remember the tomatoes. I loved her peppernuts each Christmas.

She was never one to waste anything. Often when our family would stop in, she would have a frozen milk carton full of bones and other food scraps for our cats and dogs to feast on.

She loved music and served her Lord by playing for a weekly program in the nursing home. She was also very faithful to grandpa in visiting him and taking care of him when he had Alzheimer's. Someone once asked her if she ever regretted marrying him and she said "No". They had ten great years together that she wouldn't trade for anything. I think that impacted me quite a bit.

I remember in her last years when she was in Lutheran Towers and I was already married. She made us feel special and appreciated it when Lorn and I would visit. She accepted him quickly as part of the gang."

Jan Kroeker Gieck

***

"One thing I will always remember about my grandmother is that no matter how many grandchildren she had she always made you feel special on your birthday and when you would visit her.

Dana Penner 2000

***

My memories of Grandma stretch back some 20 years now, I guess. Strangely enough they often revolve around the old house in Saskatoon. Was it on Avenue J? Looking back, I suppose it was a fairly small house but at the time it was a terrific place to explore and play games in. Christmas was often the time we visited and some memories are still vibrantly colorful: Tammy and I hiding from Dana and Gerri in the pantry downstairs, the four of us grandkids sleeping on the floor in front of the Christmas tree on Christmas Eve, walking to church on cold Sunday mornings with my Mother, wondering how my younger aunts could negotiate the slippery sidewalks in their high heels.

Childhood memories are a funny thing. I think children remember most, however, the people who genuinely took an interest in their lives at the time. The people who went beyond asking you how you liked school and who your favorite teacher was. This was Grandma.

When no one wanted to play dominoes anymore with a nine-year-old, Grandma did. She always wanted to know what's new and why you're excited about it. The characteristic I most admire in my grandmother is her commitment and dedication to family. I recall as a youngster how I was made to feel important in her eyes. I recall the same feeling as a 25 year old when she tangibly showed her love by coming to my wedding with Cheri. It was very special to us that she would come early so that she could meet Cheri beforehand and even attend one of her showers. Deeds like that are not forgotten. This type of thoughtfulness is the characteristic I'd most like to see continue in our lives. We love you very much Grandma.

Howard and Cheri Wiens

***

PHIL. 1:3 "I THANK MY GOD UPON REMEMBRANCE OF YOU".

Dear Grandma,

I'm writing this letter to tell you how much I love you and to wish you a happiest 80th birthday since I cannot be with you to tell you in person (although I'd love to!).

You are truly a special person and have touched many people's lives, including my own. God's love always shines through you.

Some of the things I remember best about you are coming over to your house numerous times. Coming for Christmas to eat turkey dinner, playing with our cousins and opening presents at your house have always been a highlight of every Christmas season.

I also remember you and Grandpa driving to our house to visit in the fall.

One of the things I have always appreciated most about you is the openness of your home. I always felt welcome when I came. You often had other visitors whom you also welcomed with open arms.

Another thing I really appreciate (especially now that I'm a little older), is the verses and words of encouragement inside all of your Christmas and birthday cards. Those few but simple words mean so much.

One thing that amazes me about you is that you never seem to forget anyone's birthday. With so many grandchildren, I don't know how you do it.

I think one of the times that is most precious to me (I'm sure it always will be), is the time when I was babysitting for Aunt Melita and you came and picked me up from the bus station and took me out for dinner. That really meant a lot to me. I appreciated it so much. That is a part of my life that I will always cherish.

You care so much about everyone! It's such an encouragement to see. I guess you are kind of a role model to me. You're just an amazing person.

I really regret not being able to be there with you on your special day but I want to wish you the best and I hope you have a great time. Since you have taken me and my family out for many meals, the next time I come to Saskatoon, I want to take you out for dinner, as my birthday present to you.

So anyways, have a happy 80th and I hope you have a great year! I plan to be there for your 90th birthday!!!

> With Much Love
> Barbara Kroeker

***

JUSTIN AND JONATHAN (1990) REMEMBER:

- Grandma and Grandpa meeting us at the door with hugs and kisses to welcome us home for Christmas.
- Christmas brunches at the Sands Hotel.
- Presents on the Christmas tree, especially looking for the little "hot wheels" cars wrapped on the tree.
- PEPPERNUTS!!
- Brown bread and rhubarb jam
- The kid's table at family gatherings so that we didn't have to be bored with adult conversation.
- Big, warm cozy blankets (only at Grandma's)!
- Playing CARREFOUR for hours in the summer of '85
- Beating us a bowling.
- Viewing the farm in Glenbush, being caught in the barn in a rainstorm. What a smell!
- Going up the Calgary Tower.
- Mini-golf on 8th Avenue in Saskatoon.
- Telephone calls on our birthdays.
-

***

THINGS I LIKE AND REMEMBER ABOUT GRANDMA:

Playing penny dominos – such fun!!!
Walking to the "Queenie"
Always remembering my birthday even though there are
lots of other people.
Generous and caring
Always friendly
Always paying attention to you
Always happy – don't ever remember Grandma sad.
Candy at Christmas!!!

A very nice person,
Happy Birthday Grandma!

Love
Jason
- 1990

***

Grandma

By Erin Friesen
Age 11

G– Gold is what reminds me of you,
R - Rubies and Roses also do too.
A – Affectionate is how you always are to me,
N – Nice and caring are two words that are in your cup of tea.
D – Deciding how to make me glad,
M – Must have made you frustrated just a tad.
A – All the times you thought of me, was all I could ask for in ETERNITY.

Grandma, there are a lot of things I remember about you. I remember how loving and caring you were to me. Some events that I remember that show this love would be when we would play Skipbo or Rumicube together. Or other times when we went in the back yard and picked gooseberries together. I also remember how calm you were when we were in the rush hour traffic and my cousin had to go to the bathroom really bad. You didn't worry about anything even though you could have missed your plane to go back home. I remember how you always were fun to be with, from playing miniature golf to going out to dinner. You always made things that are usually boring come alive and turn them into things that are really fun. Whenever our plane landed in Saskatoon, I could never wait to see you and to see what kind of fun things we would do this time.

Thanks for all the wonderful memories and thanks for always being so loving, caring and a WONDERFUL Grandma! I Love You!

Happy Birthday!!

Love,
Erin Friesen

***

My most vivid memory about Grandma is when our family flew to Saskatchewan for Christmas. I would much rather have stayed at the farm playing with Heather, Barb, Jan and Nadine toward the end of our stay, but my Mom said I had to stay at Grandma's house for the last two days.

I didn't know how to play many card games, so you, Grandma taught Mom, Nadine and me how to play Skipbo. Right away I fell in love with the game and played a lot of it in those days.

You just simply knew how to make those last few days as enjoyable as she could. Since we only visit Saskatchewan every so often, my memories are short but special.

I love you Grandma,
Kendra - 1990

***

To A Special Person
By Nadine Kapplehoff

I remember the last summer I went to see you. You and Grandpa took us out for pizza. We also ate in the basement with bread, butter and jam. I also remember reading Tiny Tim and sleeping in the basement. And playing Skipbo late at night. She sent us cards at Christmas time and for our birthdays.

She also let me know that she was very proud of me when I entered the Army in 2000.

Happy Birthday Grandma

***

"When I think of who she was, I'm just always amazed at how much love she could give, and how she was able to keep track of all of the family - especially prior to the days of emails. I know that when I have a family, I will stop at nothing short of trying to give what has been given to me."

Jonathan Parris - 2004

***

"My grandma was a woman of phenomenal strength. She never ever gave up. She always turned to God for everything. Even in the last days of her life, she'd sit at her piano and praise God with the old hymns. In my eyes, she was an incredible woman.

She was always ready to make you feel very welcome every time you came to visit her. She'd bring out the cookies and cards, so us kids could enjoy ourselves and have a lot of fun. When I look back at her life, I feel encouraged to always trust God in every circumstance and to seek the joy of the Lord at all times. When you do, He will bless you as much as He blessed My Grandma."

Leah Kudel - 2004

***

My most prominent memory I have of Grandma is of playing Skip Bo with her. I also have memories of her knitted slippers and blankets. Her house was always a great place to visit. I looked forward to visiting every Christmas. She would tie goodies to the Christmas tree, always have gingersnaps ready to eat and would always have candy for us in her candy dish.

I only really know Grandma as a kid and young teenager so she didn't get to meet Danica. I guess I didn't really get to know her that well. I wish this hadn't been the case. I wish she could have been at my wedding but one thing I knew about her for sure. It's that she loved us and she showed it. Even with what seems like thousands of children, grandchildren and great grandchildren, I still noticed that she loved me and cared for me, even if I was a brat at time.

Matthew Funk - 2004

***

My Memories of times spent with Grandma

Gooseberry jam cookies! Yum!! Don't forget those wonderful pfeffernuesse a Christmas time.

Grandma and Grandpa Abe Marten's beautiful wedding – what started out as a sort of secretive courtship turned into a real family event. I will always remember the Wiens family filling the choir loft.

I loved listening to Grandma play the piano, she was so talented. Another one of her talents was crocheting. I remember so vividly the day she showed me all the beautiful afghans she had made. We laid them all out on top of a bed and then I was allowed to pick one out for myself. There were so many!

I remember hours of playing card, board games and dominoes. Grandma was always so patient and so much fun. There were the walks around the neighborhood and special lunches at the Saskatoon Inn.

But my most precious and special memory of time spent with Grandma was sitting in the kitchen in the evening drinking Postum or was it Ovaltine. She would take these quiet times to tell me all about Grandpa Peter Wiens and the farm. Grandma would also take this time to let me know how much she loved the Lord and of the importance of having a relationship with Him.

Grandma was truly a very special lady!!

Tamara Penner Goodwin – 2004

When I think of my Grandma, there is no better way to describe her than by calling her my friend. Being one of the youngest grandchildren, I did not know her the way the others did. To me however, my Grandma was someone who would save you all the toys from her cereal boxes.

She would let you eat as much candy as you wanted from her bird shaped candy bowl. Words cannot describe who my Grandma was to me, but through the words of my heart, I dedicate this poem to her.

Grandma Martens
No words can describe
From music to love
Which transformed her insides.

When we all got together
Small gatherings? No way
Eating around a ping pong table
After a tournament of play.

Doing skits and singing songs
Was a tradition we'd never leave
Just to open one present
On the night of Christmas Eve

When we laughed and when we giggled
Was a pleasure to me
Yet she would be the one
That started the he he's

From her organ to cards
Skipbo I'd play
Beating everyone
On a really good day

Now deep in my heart,
She was a loving friend to me
But forever my Grandma
Who helped me create amazing memories.

Kristina Kudel
2004

***

Grandma's love had no boundaries. She was understanding and patient.
Grandma always took time to listen and give advice when needed. She told me that
she would have been happy to die in Sadie's place instead of Sadie. She said Sadie's
job on earth was done and it was her time to go back to God. I may not understand it
now but would someday. She was the first one to hold Caydon when he was born. I
will never forget the look on her face as she cuddled him.

She had her priorities in order. She always put God first. Grandma never judged
anyone but had an open mind. She was strong. This is a strength I strive to attain.
She was on top of things and stayed knowledgeable. She understood everything from
politics and money to the simple day-to-day tasks. Grandma laughed at my jokes, even
if they were not funny.

These are the things that come to mind when I think of her. She was special to
spend time with and gave me great advice. Grandma always had a positive side to
even my negative thoughts. Her smile and walks will always be remembered by me
and my family. Kain thought she was very special.

I miss her a lot and miss phoning her.

Heather Willems Wiggins
2004

***

The Children Remember

Mom & Dad

The Wiens children in November, 2000
Back row: L to R: Reuben, John, Herb
Middle row: L to R: Ed, Lily, Naomi, Vic
Front Row: L to R: Beth, Melita, Dina, Rose

Maria Wiens
1975

"Love is patient, Love is kind.
It does not envy, it does not boast, it is not proud.
It is not rude, it is not self seeking,
it is not easily angered, it keeps no record of wrongs.
Love does not delight in evil but rejoices in the truth.
It always protects, always trusts, always hopes, always perseveres."

I Corinthians 13:4-7 (NIV)

Happy 80th Birthday Mom,

Thank you for always being there for us. Always having time for us, listening to us about our complaints and joys.

Thank you for teaching us to work, which has made life much easier for us. When I went for my different jobs, it was not hard to please my boss. I saw how different it was for some kids - that they had to be taught how to work. It was hard for them.

Thank you for the example you and Dad were to us. I often look back at how you and Dad loved each other. How you handled different situations, which were sometimes very difficult showed how well you and Dad worked together. You worked like a giant team.

Most of all, thank you for teaching and showing us the way to God. After all that is the most important thing in life we live for. It is great how God led you and Dad through the hard times and how God helped you. After Dad was gone you kept on trusting Him. Thank you for encouraging me when I wanted to give up. You told me to keep trusting in God and to let Him guide me.

Thank you for praying for us and our children. God has answered your prayers. It is very special to me how you how your love and care in doing little things for our children. I always enjoyed the sing along times we had at home. I really have missed that a lot. I enjoyed playing games. You and Dad played a lot of different games with us, especially ball on Sunday afternoon. That meant a lot to me that you would play with us.

It's been special to Lawrence and me to go out sight-seeing, going out for meals and different functions. We have been very fortunate to do a lot of things together. Thank you for being my Mom. I love you very much.

> Your daughter
> Lily

***

Hi Mom,

Congratulations on your 80th birthday. May you have many more healthy ones to come!

Today is a very momentous occasion. Many people don't have the blessing of celebrating their 80th birthday.

When I reach back into my memory bank, I come up with cold chicken. I remember my favorite meals were cold canned chicken right out of the jar! I can taste it right now. The food was always plentiful and very delicious. It was your cooking skills, Mom, that I'm sure everyone is most grateful for. Some of us show it in different ways.

Another memory I have is your administrative skills. I'm still amazed how you kept the whole family organized and going in the same direction day after day. Yet we would always be the first at church on Sunday. With all the work to get the family ready, we should have been the last, but no, most of the time we were one of the first to arrive, thanks to your great skills of running a major corporation. Saskatchewan Telephone should have hired you to run their business or better still, Canada Post still needs you to organize it.

I remember your eternal optimism the most. You always laughed about any problem. You have influenced me very much that way. You have been most influential in my life in your devotion and trust in God. I'm sure we all must say that. I want to especially thank you for your non-judgmental love towards me in difficult times. Thank you for standing by me without judgment in my marital life. Even when I was failing and rebelling, you showed great love and care. I thank you for that.

May God reward and bless you richly for all you have taught us and given to us in your abundant love and prayers on our behalf. Thanks for being a true MOTHER.

Love,

Herb

***

A TRIBUTE TO THE GREATEST MOM!

Putting thoughts down on paper – what a job! Many go through my mind, but what should I put down on paper or how should I express myself?

Mother, memories of many years ago and memories of not so long ago – "Faithfulness" in little things and big – never letting us down, ready to listen. Breakfast on the table – hot ones at that – not that I ever liked porridge – I hated it – but it was good for you, especially "Sunnyboy" – which was much better than "puffed wheat". Mother was always there when we came home from school. How different when she wasn't, especially when we found out she was in a hospital. Mothers never get sick!

Her days were long and demanding I'm sure; never complaining, at least not where you could hear her. I'm sure she had many reason to complain what with so many little ones around. She went about daily living with that 'quiet spirit'. I often wondered how she never allowed anything to upset her or get the best of her. She was strong. I'm sure her inner strength came from the Lord, where else? Physically she was a slender lady not built for the pioneer life in no man's land.

I remember a loving caring Mother. One who always had a smile for you – an encouraging word and a gentle touch. However she could also be stern – demanding or expecting the best from you. Chores had to be done well and complete. You truly had to admire her for 'managing a large busy household' plus a large garden - organizing responsibilities and tasks for everyone from the youngest to the oldest. Mother was a great overseer. Tasks not done well had to be done a second time. Our best was always expected – no ifs or buts. It did seem astonishing how she managed to get us all up in the mornings, have morning chores done prior to breakfast than have the house clean and tidy before we left for school at 8 AM. Some hustle and bustle went on, I assure you. Tardiness was not accepted, and for sure not late for school.

We operated in crews to accomplish things – milking crews, dishwashing crews, bed making (each his own), and floor washing crew. I assure you, you never saw a house-cleaning job accomplished so quickly and efficiently and out the door on your way to school on time. Mother and Dad had to be good motivators. I'm sure she breathed a sigh of relief when all the right people were out the door with only a few left behind.

Mother was a hard worker, even though we all had tasks and responsibilities. There was little time for rocking except when feeding a baby. Mom was always busy lovingly sewing for us. Yes, she was a great seamstress, drawing her own patterns. Find a picture in Eaton's catalogue and she would sew it for you. Patching worn out clothes was a continuous job as was remaking things. Holes in clothing were not acceptable – neither were dirty ones. Washdays were a wonder in themselves. No electricity – can you imagine the job? Mondays – regular as clockwork it was washday.

Somebody was elected to miss school and help – I never minded missing school on Mondays even though I would have to work hard. It was a rather special day with Mom. Can you imagine washing clothes for a baseball team or a small army all in one day? Remember there was no electricity or running water.

Hospitality – our table was never too small. There was always room for one more. Dear old Chester – our very own hermit – always knew when mealtime was at our house. She never minded having this strange old man with the long beard come by. There were many others who shared our mealtimes with us. She was never too busy to help another person – whether neighbor, relative or stranger.

Serving was another attribute. Playing piano was a great gift God had given her, and she used it to His glory. Many evenings I would peacefully go to sleep listening to Mom play piano. Music just flowed from her fingers. She played for many years for the church choir and congregations. Many hours were spent around the piano singing songs – she wasn't only a pianist but also a singer.

I know I have only mentioned the early years of her life but I know her many attributes have carried on to later years for I know she is still a very loving caring person and continues to be a shining light for all of us. I could write a few more pages but will allow someone else to cover a few other periods of history.

Ever loving you,

Rose

***

A Tribute to My Mother

Thank you, Lord for a Mother who cares
About each of her children equally well.
But in particular, a Mother who tried to
Understand when I felt I was not being understood.
Thank you, Lord, for a Mother who loves,
Even when her love is not being returned.
Her heart was always open to hear
What I had to say in spite of our differences.
Thank you, Lord, for a Mother who prays
For all her children day by day.
Her faith in you, Lord, when times were tough
Has helped me know I too can depend on you.
Thank you, Lord, for a Mother who shares
Her time, talents and blessings.
Her generosity has spurned me on
To live for others as you have planned.

With Love,

Anna

Happy 80ᵗʰ birthday Mom.

How does one write a tribute to a Mother like you? I find this rather difficult. Not that there is nothing to write but rather how to write what one feels about his Mother.

I do not know how anyone could have had a more adequate Mother. You were so proficient in so many ways. I suppose what I admire or see the most in you, is your absolute trust in God that things will work out. Obstacles were many but you always faced them undaunted. I certainly hope I have inherited your strong spirit to carry things through.

I admire the way you accept tasks and then simply do them. You have always seemed to be able to prioritize what is important and needed to be done, and then were not distracted from doing the job. I know you worried some, but the worries and concerns never seemed to paralyze your efforts. I really admire you for the things you find and found to do to help others. You certainly weren't too proud to find employment where it was available. I still find it amazing how you could manage your financial affairs so well when you left Glenbush with so little and yet lived so well!

I would hope and wish that when I'm 80 years old, I will be able to look back on my life with as much satisfaction as I think you should.

Reuben

***

For the approximately twenty years that I have known Mom, I have appreciated and admired many of her qualities. I marvel at how she can go through life, accepting the ups and downs, in a matter of fact manner with very few complaints. She is such a steady and thorough person that the decisions she makes are wise ones.
She's also able to ask for help and other people's opinions when needed. Whenever Mom doesn't necessarily approve of a person's actions or beliefs, she still is able to accept that person as someone worth caring about. I also appreciate the way that Mom has always made us feel welcome when come to visit.

Sharon Wiens

***

When I think of Mom, many wonderful images come to mind. Images of ready smile and helping arms. Of the joy she took in preparing for our Christmases and Easters. As Christmas neared, we would look through the catalogues again and again, making our wish lists and dreaming our dreams. Then in early December, I think it was, Mom and Dad would closet themselves in the living room and order our presents through the catalogue mail order system. A few weeks later, huge boxes would arrive at the train station. Now the real speculations would begin. When we sang the line "the hopes and fears of all the years are met in thee tonight", I thought it was referring just these apprehensive speculations.

One of my pleasant Easter memories involves Mom's excellent Easter bread or Paska. I remember one afternoon I was out wading in the spring floods among the willows close to the farmyard. I enjoyed teasing the nesting Horned Grebes; and was as usual, trying to see how close to the tope of my boots I could let the water come, without wetting the insides... and always going just one step too far. When I got home, trying not to let Mom see my wet socks, I could smell that wonderful aroma of freshly baked Paska. Mom sliced one or two of the loaves for supper, and I doubt that anything ever tasted better than that!

My very favorite memories of Mom revolve around her love of Music. How I loved it when she played the piano and Dad sang. I can still remember the feeling of gemutlichkeit that enveloped me as I lay in bed and heard them go through song after song. I would always be disappointed when the music stopped. I'm sure I must have had beautiful dreams those nights.

I also loved it when they got together with some of the neighbors and Dad got down his guitar or autoharp, Mom on the piano, Mr. Zimmerman brought his violin and the Borns played their mandolins. It was fun listening to them, and it never bothered me if things were in tune or not. Unfortunately, as I recall, this orchestra didn't last too long.

Another aspect of Mom and Dad's music making which I enjoyed very much was their, and later, our participation in the music at church. I will never forget sitting in the front bench as a boy; looking up and seeing Dad sing a solo or a duet with Peter Pauls. I thought then that someday I would like to be able to sing like that. I thank Mom for her help towards that end. During the winter after Dad passed away, with the younger kids at school, Mom and I were alone. She would sometimes call me to the piano and we would spend many hours going through the old hymns found in the Gesangbuch.

Thank you, Mom, for all the musical, emotional and financial help you have given me to enable me to carry on as a musician.

Love
Ed

***

Dear Mom,

I remember the first time we met. I waited for you, excited and nervous, at the Toronto Airport, back in the fall of 1983. Emily was a babe-in-arms; Ed had to work that evening, and I was attempting to figure out which passenger looking for her luggage might be you.

After what seemed a long time, I spotted you, and at the same instant, you spotted us. As we met that first time, you hugged me, and then in one deft motion, swept Emily into your arms. She took to you at once. So did I.

Happy 80th birthday, Mom.

How I wish we could be there to join in the celebration.

Love.

Donna Wiens

***

I REMEMBER YOU:

• Helped my learn to read and listened patiently as I stumbled over words and taught me to print my name in straight letters.

• Taught me to play piano and encouraged me to practice and practice by giving me time to play daily before supper instead of pumping water. What a motivation!

• Made Reuben, Ed and I go without freshly baked "Paska" on Easter Saturday because we had taken a short cut through the slough area and got our feet and boots soaking wet. You were not happy at our thoughtlessness.

• Gave me my last "lickin'" for taking a detour to check my gopher traps enroute to getting Dad and the boys from the stone-pickin' field in time for dinner. Dinner was waiting!

• Spent many hours designing dress patterns from pictures in the catalogues and sewing made to measure clothes of all kinds at the sewing machine for all of us.

• Bargained with store managers in North Battleford to get me the coats I wanted at a more affordable price.

• Spent hours listening to our clothing needs and wants, completing catalogue orders, and making the family allowance checks of $80 pay for clothes for 14 children.

• Encouraged me to go to Business College, University to get an education rather than just get another job.

• Encouraged me to be independent in buying my first car even though my brothers, especially Reuben, discouraged it as it might ruin my last chance for marriage. In fact, you even gave me a generous loan towards it, trusting my ability to repay.

• Telephoned from London, England at midnight and asked, "Has my passport arrived?" The answer was "No". However, you made it all the way to Rome before the authorities said "No further!" However, after they issued a temporary passport, you traveled successfully to Israel, almost drowned in the Dead Sea; but thankfully, you arrived home safely. In spite of all the setbacks on this your first trip overseas, you never lost your sense of adventure in travel!

• Traveled with me to the Black Hills, South Dakota.

• Expressed great surprise at Dina announcing my engagement to John Parris when I came home at Christmas, 1971, without a ring and a fiancée (just a slide). Blondina announced, "Guess what! Vi's engaged!" Your response, "To what, her teaching?"

WE REMEMBER YOU

• Waited up well past midnight and welcomed four "hippie-looking friends" into your home to spend the night.

• Made July 8, 1972 a truly memorable and enjoyable wedding day.

• Welcomed newcomers into the family despite accent and name.

• Helped us buy our first bedroom furniture and our first house. You were always willing to lend us money. (With interest, of course!)

- Drove to Kitimat with us in our pickup truck, and slept in the back of the truck while we were in the tent. John spent a few anxious moments in the middle of the night until he realized the noise was not a prowling bear but the truck suspension creaking as you turned in your sleep.
- Came to Kitimat when Justin was born and spent most of the week baking cookies as Justin spent an extra week in the hospital.
- Showed us how to travel in Europe for six weeks in 1973 with only a shoulder bag for luggage, after our borrowed VW van was stolen in Paris.
- Demonstrated real fortitude at age 62 sitting in the backseat of a little Renault 5 all the way from Paris to Barcelona and back.
- Mailed us a certain letter in the summer of 1976 filled with the excitement of a young teenager meeting a special someone in her life.

CHARACTERISTICS WHICH WE APPRECIATE:

- EVERYTHING!! (Jonathan's immediate answer).
- A fun and caring Grandmother with a warm and kind voice.
- Not being judgmental about friends, no matter how questionable in appearance or what nationality.
    - Through IVCF Vi had many contacts with African and East Indians students, most of them male.
- Although you must sometimes have been concerned, you always supported our decisions such as my going to Terrace, B.C. in 1963 or to Europe for the summer of 1967.
- Steadfast and loyal to family and friends.
- Strong in faith. You lived it more than talked about it.
- You never fell apart in the fact of difficulty but remained emotionally self-controlled.
- You always looked forward to the future rather than spent time living in the past. You did not wish me to stay home another year after Dad died because you felt strongly that life must go on.
- A feminist in your own way who believed that a boys' presence was also important in the dish pit!
- Not domineering or critical of grandchildren's behaviors and dislikes, having a childproof house, and being able to bear grandchildren's tears.

I would take it as a tremendous compliment should anyone else say, "You're just like your Mother!" We thank you for being YOU, our Mother and Grandmother.

John and Vi Parris

Dear Mom:

In reaching down into the barrel of the past, it is certainly not necessary to grasp for such unbecoming things as flattery and insincere words to prepare a tribute to you, our Mother. We can easily and truly bring up beautiful, lively and honest memories, of which there are plenty.

In the United States, the president's wife is referred to as the "First Lady". Ever since I have become familiar with that term, you have uncategorically been that to me. You have been the shining role model for me, but kindly not attained perfection. That would have left too formidable a shadow for me to follow. Because of your joyful and peaceful self-acceptance, even though you have not found or displayed yourself as perfect, you have rolled out the red carpet for us to do the same for ourselves. As your children, who have seen you at your best and your worst, we only find it difficult to write our tributes because there is so much to put into such small insignificant packages as words and phrases.

The first thing that comes to my mind when I look back, Mom, is presence. You had (and still have) presence. That is why I never liked to come into our house as a child unless you were in it. There was a certain security I felt if you were there; that life would hold together and we would be cared for. You may not know it, but I still carry your presence with me. In my mind, you talk to me, reassure me and urge me on countless times each day. Thank you for that.

That you were wise and insightful was demonstrated to me the time I was probably 9 or 10. Remember the pennies we got for catching a gopher and presenting the tail all fluffy and dripping with blood? Well on one of those busy Monday morning wash days, just as you were busily stuffy hot steaming laundry through the wringer, I popped my hand through the nearby kitchen window, holding a foxtail weed, feeling you certainly wouldn't notice the difference between that and a gopher tail. I was duly impressed that you weren't fooled for a second.

Another time I had been given a certain amount of time to be in bed, but because of worthy distractions I had a hard time managing this. When I heard your footsteps coming up the stairs, I was sure you wouldn't spank me if you found me kneeling at my bedside praying. Of course, you let me finish my prayer but unhappily, I couldn't con my way out of disciplinary action.

You were wise in how you cared for us and also in how you let us go. I have always valued the freedom you gave us in becoming independent and our own persons. I don't think I can ever remember you comparing me to any other of my siblings and wondering why I wasn't like them.

You were ever and always, it seemed to me, completely efficient and capable to accomplish whatever you set to do. How you have inspired me to push myself beyond the brink or at least to the edge. I am sure you have no idea how many times you speak to me, in my memory or conscience, to get out there and try and try again.

Thousands of times I have heard you say to me in my mind, "If there is a will, there is a way!" You and Dad both taught us not to be afraid of fear, or to let it paralyze us, but to press on in spite of, and many times WHEN we were fearful. I can still see you shaking your fist with conviction saying that "When it gets tough, you CANNOT give us, but you HAVE to get out there and fight!"

Your efficiency and capabilities were seen in such things as running the farm after Dad's death, meticulously keeping track of your finances, and managing a household of 16, baking, sewing, gardening and teaching us the art of self-sufficiency, yet still having time to read many of the books we brought home from school, as well as taking an afternoon nap everyday.

You took pleasure in your children's accomplishments. I remember how nice it felt to have you be present at our sports days and I think I could run a little faster and jump a little farther when you were there to encourage us on and to smile proudly at our attempts to win the prize.

But of course, your courage and trust, your strong fighting spirit, which was just as gentle and quiet in nature was most obvious and most severely tried when your husband and our Dad was suddenly gone. I will never forget the precise moment when I was in the dining room watching you wipe the table after the evening meal, turning to me and gently stating that you were very sure that God had a very good reason for taking Daddy now and that it was most likely for his good. Such a positive way to react to such a painful experience! Even though I saw tears, never did I hear you complain about our loss, nor did I perceive a bitter spirit of resentment and self-pity.

You had a wonderful sense of humor and it was always good to hear you laugh. I remember so well the day I learned my ABC's. I was working on them so hard that when I knelt to say my evening prayers at your feet and started to repeat the ABC's instead of my prayers, you giggled and laughed uncontrollably. I felt completely good; a little silly yes, but very good.

Another thing I have always appreciated and admired about you is your love of beauty and appreciation for beautiful things such a racehorses, sunsets and music. Ah, music! What a heritage you gave us and what a pleasure hearing you play the piano with such feeling, such joy and love. Your love of God and all that is good and beautiful came from flowing out of your fingers like cool summer evening breezes.

Just the other day Naomi showed me the graduation card I had sent her. I didn't even remember I had given her one. I read it and thought that the poem on it, which was written to a girl and was fashioned after Rudyard Kipling's "IF" was totally idealistic and completely unattainable. Then I read it again and realized that NO! it was not unattainable because Mom, it was rather close to describing you. It was written in the "If you can be... tense but I found that I could write it in the past tense about you something like this:

YOU

You have been a girl and gloried in it,
Because it was the place for you to fill,
You have been a lady every minute,
Yet taken sporting chances with a will;
You have held your temper when you were ruffled,
And forced a smile when frowns were hovering near,
And kept the burning tongue of scandal muffled
By shielding those you hold so dear.

You have followed styles and worn them sweetly,
But let not what you spent outweigh your brain,
You have won some goal you've sought completely
Yet knew that broader reaches still remain;
You have looked on modern fads and notions
And found them good, but never played the fool,
You have understood all deep emotions
And yet not put your life beneath their rule:

You have waited with patience when it was needful,
Yet kept no person waiting for yourself,
And of all others' troubles have been most heedful,
But have hidden your own sad stories on the shelf;
You have worked each day and still been plucky,
Or lived in wealth, but wore no haughty pride,
You have counted yourself as mighty lucky
And had a friend at all times by your side:

You have dreamt but not sat idly longing,
Or played with ease, yet found some work to do,
You have still had faith when doubts were thronging,
And been the friend you'd have one be to you;
You have loved with all the soul that's in you
And let the world no selfish motive see,
And nothing less than what was best could win you –
And so you've been the one God meant for to be!

And as the finishing touch, I'd like to tie a ribbon onto my gift of tribute to you, by saying that one of the nicest things I choose to believe God did for me, besides giving me the gift of life and then of eternal life, was to choose you of the millions of women on earth to be MY MOTHER!

Congratulations on attaining your 80th birthday. This world needs more people like you!

    Love,
    Beth

***

Dear Mom,

  On this your eightieth birthday I would like to sincerely praise God for you and let you know that your life has been a great blessing. I wanted so badly to be able to come and celebrate with you.

  When I think back to the first time I was at your place in Glenbush, to be introduced to "Beth's Family", I think that the strongest impression that I was left with was of acceptance. You had a way of welcoming me that was open and nonjudgmental.

  Through the years whenever Beth and I have been able to come and spend time with you (which is far too seldom) you have always taken us in with love and affection. Too often we take that for granted, especially in today's world.

There are many people who have never experienced that kind of attitude even once. I truly am fortunate to have become part of your family.

  Yours with a thankful heart

  Ernie Friesen

***

Mother may I Bless You with the following thoughts:

There are a few things that I would like to share with my Mother that I remember that really bless me about you!

You and Dad never argued in front of us children; this is something I must work on.

Thank you for teaching us to pray and know that all our needs are met Jesus Our Lord.

Thank you for your consistent discipline in my early life.

One thing that always amazed me was that whenever I came home unannounced you would always say you were thinking about me and it never seemed to be a surprise at all. This of course is because I know you always kept all of us in your prayers. Thank you for your many prayers for me.

I remember the first time you came and visited me in Vancouver when I was living in a community home where we ministered to street kids; you were right in there sharing and ministering to the kids in our home. Thank you for the caring heart you have for us and those in need.

Thank you Mom for teaching us how to work and giving us such a rich heritage which I am sure is the reason I've never been out of work for any period of time.

It really blesses Marj and me that you never forget to call us on or around our birthday. It shows that you care about our welfare and it shows us that God is still caring for us through you.

So now I pray that you've reached this milestone of three score and twenty year which is a true sign of the Lord's favor on you, may the Lord Jesus richly bless you in the remaining years He has allotted for you.

I love you very much and Thank You for being My Mother through the good times I gave you as well as the many concerns I gave. I appreciate the fact that you always stood with me as your son John.

> Much Love
> John Wiens

***

Mom, I do not know you as well, being one of the recent additions to the family. The thing I have noticed the most about you is the acceptance you have of other people coupled with a genuine interest in what they are doing.

Within the family bonds you have children fellowshipping within a wide spectrum of Christian doctrines, yet you accept each one where they are, discussing and sometimes arguing with them over issues, yet never leaving them with the feeling that you are disappointed in them for not following the same beliefs in which they were brought up in. I find this totally amazing in a person from your generation.

Your letters and phone calls are unique, since you spend the time finding out what we and others you know are doing and they are always a lift to our spirits. Thank you for your genuine interest in us as a family.

Marjorie Wiens

***

Dear Mom:

As we get older for some reason we always, or hopefully, seem to remember a lot of the good that has happened in our lives and forget the bad, if there is any to forget. In your case Mom, as far as I'm concerned there is no bad to remember.

When I think back to childhood, I remember you as a quiet, loving and caring person - someone who loved each one of her children equally as much.

I remember one time after realizing your light always seemed to be on until very late at night, I asked you if you always slept with the light on. You replied, no, you were awake. Then I asked, "How can you stay awake so late so often, and what do you do so you don't get frustrated from not falling asleep?" You told me that you spent a lot of your time praying for each of us. That answer has had a very good long-term effect on my life.

I want to thank you for all that you have done for me and the positive influence you have had in my life.

Thank You Mom

Your Son,

Victor "love you"

***

Some of my favorite memories of Mom are of her visits to us when Ryan and Joel were young. The visit I remember the best, was the one to Vernon when George and I had just moved there and lived in a house close to Kalamalka Lake. Mom always had some handiwork with her so she seemed quite content to spend parts of the day working on one creation or another, allowing me to carry on with what seemed necessary in what I thought was quite a busy household.

In retrospect, when I compare my two child family with her family of 14, I'm sure she must have wondered at times, whatever made me think I had my hands full! She never gave that impression, though, but she might have been thinking that or even laughing just a little behind her hand. Instead she left me with the feeling that I was doing a good job as a wife and mother. For that, I thank you today, Mother Martens.

Mom Martens has to be one of the very few women who know how to show support as a mother and mother-in-law without interfering. Even after a few days spent in our home, I'm convinced that although she observed instances of parenting and choices of spending our money that she might have felt critical of, she allowed us to make our own mistakes and "do it our way". Mom, you must have had a sore tongue from having to bite it so often!

One of the greatest gifts, though, that Mom has given to Ryan, Joel and me, is the love and open arms she extended to Hal as my new husband and Ryan and Joel's new dad. For the past ten years she has affirmed our marriage in word and deed. Hal and I have so often felt incredulous at her continued gestures of love and acceptance over these past years. Mom, you have shown so much courage and selflessness to us – thank you – we love you very much.

Edith (Wiens) Toews

***

Many things come to mind when I think of you, Mom and how you impacted my own life. At this point I am exactly half your age and I hope that when I reach 80 I am as successful in life as you and can look back with few regrets.

I can still see you kneading your weekly batch of bread which sometimes ended in a fight to see who would get the first hot crust of bread. I can still smell the freshly cut bread with butter melting on the top. It tasted so good with all that melted butter.

Christmas was always special. When you room was off limits we knew that Christmas near especially when we brought home all those mysterious packages from the post office on the bus. We would just die of curiosity to see what was in them. Your Christmas preparations consumed much of your time with the making of all those candies, cookies and Christmas cakes. How we loved those rare yearly treats but especially I loved those marshmallows covered candies covered with coconut. No one could rival your baking. It was the time of year when we got to devour Japanese oranges and Halvah. Some of those childhood memories have become a tradition in our home today.

Your cooking was always so good that I guess I was never interested in learning to cook until I really had to. I always looked forward to eating such favorites such as farmer sausage and borscht. Trying to prepare enough food and some to spare must have always been a challenge to you.

Many other values and things were equally important to you. Hospitality was one of them. It seems that in the years we lived on the farm, more often than not, there were always guests for Sunday noon dinners who were invited on the spur of the moment after church. I recall a time when I complained about my inability to host a group of people because I felt it involved preparing a proper meal and you so wisely told me that it wasn't important what was served on the table but rather what counted was the fellowship around the table. I only hope that I can learn to do that better.

Music played a big part. Many Sunday afternoons were spent around the piano. You encouraged us to memorize hymns, and even paid us a quarter for each song and Sunday school verse that we memorized. Many of those old songs that I memorized are still among my favorites and can still be sung partly without a book. That encouragement you gave us in memorizing was useful for it helped me memorize harder groups of verses much easier in more recent years.

Family was important to you. You never regretted having a large family or even coming from one. I once asked you why you had so many children. You responded with a question of your own "which ones shouldn't I have had?"

I have always appreciated it so very much that you were there when we needed you the most. I remember the time when we sent you an envelope with some checks but no letter because there was nothing to write about. You called me a week later and asked if everything was okay. Your intuition told you something was wrong.

Your influence over us has been great. You instilled in us the desire to work and kept us busy which no doubt kept us out of trouble at the same time. Many a bored summer day was spent weeding that huge garden or thinning those many rows of carrots but you also allowed time for pleasure. One day when there were relatives visiting from Ontario, we all loaded up into the back of a truck and went to Jackfish Lake for the day. One summer we even went to North Battleford to a rodeo.

Fortunately some of our wishes did not come true. One day when Uncle John Enns was visiting, he asked me what I wanted to be when I grew up. Instead of saying I wanted to be a nurse or a teacher, as he expected, I told him I wanted to be lazy. My life has not provided many chances for laziness.

You also encouraged reading. Books were always a welcome guest in our home. There were times when I would rather read a book than do housework especially on Saturday mornings which were cleanup days at home. It was such a temptation to read a book that I found lying around rather than clean the room.

Our spiritual upbringing was very important. One very vivid impression in my memory bank is the daily scene around the breakfast table. Before we even ate, Dad would always read the daily German Bible reading from his Sunday school quarterly despite the fact that some of us never understood a word of German. You continued that practice after he died but in English instead. Every evening even when we were young, you or someone else in the family read us a story and prayed with us.

You practiced the art of compromise especially after we lived in the city and attended a church half a block away from our home. Sunday school was never interesting for me but you handled this problem by telling us we didn't have to go to Sunday school but we were expected to go to church.

Even before we moved to the city, we saw how united you and Dad were. I recall a time in the old country Glenbush church where it was a custom for children to sit in the front with the women on the left and the men on the right hand side of the church. Your discipline was always consistent so that we knew where we stood in that area. If we misbehaved when sitting with our friends, we'd have to sit with you. It that didn't work, we had to sit with Dad, which sometimes came with consequences of being removed from the service for a spanking. Only once do I recall ever taking it to the bitter end and once was enough to learn that you meant what you said.

I never really understood you as a parent until I became a parent myself. I appreciated so much the time you came out to help me after Kendra was born. You showed me how to give her a bath. I want to raise my children as well as you did, instilling in them lasting values. You showed us more by example than words on how to be a good parent. Thank you Mom!

Perhaps what has influenced me more than any other thing is the way you have handled the difficult times in your life. Life has thrown you a few wicked curves but you handled them with few complaints and much courage. You gave us a gift that can never be forgotten when on the day of Dad's memorial service you permitted a family record to be cut that included the voice of Dad so that we'd know what he sounded like for years to come. Thank you for showing us how to go on even in difficult situations.

Even in your own challenges which were similar to what we have been going through, you constantly reminded me to look to the Maker rather than dwell on the problem. I have a greater understanding, empathy and appreciation for you in your own difficulties.

I admire the way you have stood by your family and loved us regardless of our mistakes and blunders. Never once have I ever heard you say "I told you so". I can only hope that I can learn to look at other people through those eyes. Thank you for showing us to control our tongues. All in all, I am proud that you are my mother and I love you so very much.

HAPPY 80TH BIRTHDAY MOTHER!

Naomi

***

11-2-90

IN HONOR OF YOUR BIRTHDAY

You have the gift of hospitality, always taking us in, giving of your time and efforts with tasty foods, clean sheets and warm fellowship.

Mother, your devotion to your Lord, family and church has kept you on course through the storms of life and provided you an anchor in changing times.

May our cry be the same as yours when Joshua cried "...As for me and my house, we will serve the Lord."

Happy Birthday Mom,

Phil Kapplehoff

***

THOUGHTS FROM ME TO YOU MOM

As a child, I always remember your softness. I cherished the times I could lay my head in your lap or on your soft shoulder in church.

As a rebellious teenager, I felt you were of another generation and frequently went my own way. Although I knew you loved me, I felt unable to please you. It was only much later in life that I realized how well you knew me and my capabilities. Never yelling at me or raising your voice was one of your admirable qualities.

Even through my rough spots in life, I never forgot the values you taught me, especially the love of God and family life. I value your great insights into reading people's characters. You were right about them all!

As I get older, I enjoy the calming effect that my visits with you have especially after a stressful day with the children. I must have you know that I need you to hug me. I cannot be afraid to hug you and tell you how much I love you.

Melita

***

Dear Mom,

There have been many times in the last few years that I've wanted to do this but I never seem to know how to start. So I guess it's good to get prodded a bit and finally do it or there will come a time when I'll regret not having written you this letter.

Mom, I've loved you for a lot of years; you have been the best Mom I could ask for. You took good care of me for so many years and helped me in so many ways. All through childhood, you took the time to teach us how to live our lives pleasing to God. A vivid memory of my childhood is the many times I saw you reading your Bible, memorizing Bible verses and praying.

You've worked so hard all your life, sometimes I feel ashamed of how lazy I get, of how little I do, compared to what you did all those years on the farm. I've always admired you for the strength you've had. When Dad died, it must have been hard to think of what you still had to do by yourself. I'm amazed you didn't break under the pressure you must have felt – what a big responsibility you had with so many of us still so young. You've done a remarkable job and shown true strength of character.

I probably wouldn't have made it through university without your help and encouragement. That first semester when I felt like quitting, your encouragement kept me going. Thank you for always stressing the importance of an education.

Thank you for the warm welcome you gave to Russ when we started dating. It was nice to have your approval of the husband I chose. And you've been so good to the kids too. Even after having so many grandchildren already, you've treated our kids like they're special. You've been very gracious to all your extended family. How do you remember everyone's birthday year after year?

Your gift of hospitality has been a real example to me. Nobody every left your house hungry. You always had food for surprise visitors. And now when we come to visit, we all still look forward to your special meals. (Those homemade noodles are the best!) The big hugs we get when we arrive are great too.

I have a lot of fond memories of growing up. I can remember very clearly the summer I spent in Jasper. I received a letter that I still have today. You said you had such shocking news I'd better lie down before I read on. That was when you told me you were seeing a man but you wouldn't tell me who it was. I had to wait a whole month to find out who it was! Talk about keeping me in suspense! I guess it's not very often that Mother and daughter get engaged within a few months of each other.

In all our moving around during our marriage, I especially enjoyed the years we lived in Saskatoon. It was so nice to be able to drop in to see you whenever I felt housebound or lonely for adult company. You welcomed us in any time and put up with a lot of noise and mischief from the kids. They always enjoyed going to Grandma's house. Matthew knew the route to your house before he was a year old. If he knew we were on our way to your house, he'd start to scream if we didn't make the turn onto Idylwyld Drive by the Travelodge.

So now Mom, as you celebrate your 80th birthday, I want to thank you for all the love, help and encouragement you've given me throughout my life. I'm sure we all hope you have many more good healthy years ahead of you.

Blondina

A POEM DEDICATED TO MARIA MARTENS

(TO MOM)

In the spring of '76, Dina's Mother I did meet
Her daughter was young and pretty and her Mom very sweet
I started courting Dina much to her Mom's dismay
She said, "Be home by midnight!" and then she'd start to pray
But I knew from the start, I really liked Dina's Mom
Cause she was warm and friendly and you know, kind of fun
She always made me feel at home whenever I came
We laughed and had a good time and she always remembered my name
She always took good care of us especially at meals
Bread and pies and kielke, ah...how good my stomach feels

And Dina and I, well we tied the knot
Cause Dina's Mom and Abe showed us they liked it a lot
And now fourteen years and two more grandkids later
I'd still give her a 10 if I was asked to rate her
And through the years we've all felt her genuine love
Cause between you and me, I think she's been touched from above
But of all the things I admire the most
Is her love for the Father, the Son and the Holy Ghost
Finally in conclusion, just let say
I love you Mom and have a great Happy Birthday

Russell R. Funk
(Favorite Manitoba Son-In-Law)

MY DAD

Dad was a man of few words. He had a kind and gentle spirit. He was a hard worker and a man of all trades. He was a farmer, engineer, butcher, and a wonderful father and very musical. He was lots of fun when he wasn't too busy with work. He enjoyed reading books in the winter. When we were small I remember Dad playing a lot with us. He was the horse and we the riders. As we grew older, he played table games with us or in the summer played ball with us.

In winter during one of my last years at home, he made a rink and skated with us. We sang together and worked together. I enjoyed working with him – feeding the cattle, horses and pigs etc. I had the privilege of building the lattice fence with Dad. That time was special. He taught me to work. I learned many things, how to do different jobs which has helped me in vocation (farming).

I had a close and good relationship with Dad. I could talk to him and he listened – sometimes giving advice. When he gave advice, he often gave the pros and cons and told us now "decide for yourself".

When Dad had to make decisions he would be in deep thought. I remember sometimes even at dinner or supper, he would hardly respond to what we were saying. He was planning the next move or how he would do things. He invented an easier way of washing clothes or separated the milk. He also made it possible for us to have running water.

The activities that Dad was involved in church were – director of the children's choir, singing in the adult choir, leading an orchestra and a ladies choir. I was privileged to sing in the ladies choir.

In the community he was on the school board for a few years. He got the power into the community and he worked hard on getting the phone in. He ran the snow plough in winter to keep the roads open. He was the butcher for the community for many summers.

I guess Dad had some influence on whom and what kind of person I married. He advised me against marrying my first boyfriend. I always wanted somebody who was somewhat like Dad – a Christian who loved Jesus, a farmer and a kind and gentle person. When I married Lawrence, I wished so much that Dad could be at our wedding and see us get married because I felt he would be very pleased.

Dad's unexpected death was something I had been wrestling with for several months before he died. I had a dream that he had died about three months before. I was so glad I was able to be home for all of August and do a lot of things with him. The night the call came, the first thing that came to mind was Dad and what had happened. I didn't want this to happen. I didn't want to believe it.

It didn't seem real until I got home from Winnipeg. It didn't really hit me that Dad was gone until the first breakfast when Dad wasn't reading the Bible before the meal. I struggled with it for a while, until a message I heard at one time came to mind. It said we are to thank God for everything even if a loved one has died. Finally I prayed and said, "Thank you God for taking Dad home to yourself" and then it was as if a burden had been lifted. I still miss him and wish many times he was here to enjoy my family and what we are doing.

You ask me, how did his life shape mine? It was his example of how he lived for Jesus. He taught us about Jesus by reading God's Word to us daily morning and evening. He took us faithfully to church and Sunday school. Through his love for music, I learned many of the hymns hearing Dad singing them at home, especially after he bought Mom the piano. He would also play the guitar or autoharp and with Mom on the piano, they'd both sing while they played.

When I said I wanted to get baptized, he prepared me for the occasion by asking me to tell him about my conversion and asked me questions as to why I wanted to be baptized and a few others just like they did in church. This helped me a lot. When I asked to go to Bible school, he encouraged me and let me go.

His example of how he and Mom worked together influenced me. They planned things out together. Dad taught Mom to do the farm accounts, income tax and made sure she knew what was all involved.

I also recall Dad and Mom going arm in arm for a walk to inspect the fields. Seeing them hold hands or Dad taking Mom on his lap gave me the assurance that they loved each other.

If I could have one last conversation with him, I would tell Dad how much I loved him. I'd thank him for being my Dad, for loving and caring for me and for teaching me many valuable lessons.

Lily Wiens Willems

***

Who was my Dad

By Herb Wiens

I remember Dad as being a fun loving, quiet, kind man even though I remember one spanking I got – I thought I was going to die. Dad had a very unique kind of quietness about him. I don't remember him saying a lot – except when he talked, you listened and he always made good common sense. He did a lot of playing with us. He taught us a lot of games – indoor and outdoor alike.

I guess the two most memorable things I liked was to work together with him; I idolized his ability to out work everybody and nothing was ever impossible. Somehow he was always able to figure everything out. If it didn't work, he would make it work. All the friends and neighbors knew that. I thought he was Superman.

When I was seventeen years old I had a tremendous need to get away from home, because I didn't want to disappoint Dad and because I knew I couldn't keep up with him in work or his standards of accomplishments. I wish I could have talked with him about that. But I couldn't express myself.

The most fun I had with Dad was around the piano. We would sing for hours; he just never seemed to get tired. He taught me a lot about the love of singing. I thought he was the greatest. I still think he really was very good having self-taught himself.

Yes, he conducted the children's choir as well as the Glenbush orchestra. He would sing for about 15 minutes with the children in church many times and at Christmas he would usually lead the children's choir for the Christmas Eve program. Dad had a very quiet but deep faith in God. He took everything to God before he made a decision.

He was definitely a pioneer. He usually was the first in the community to do things. For years he ran a beef ring which solved the problem of having fresh beef all summer long without any electricity. He bought a huge tractor to break land. People often laughed at him for his optimism but he usually had the last laugh because the next year, the other farmers usually followed his lead.

Even though I loved being with Dad and working together, we didn't seem to talk a lot. That is one thing I wish would have been different. He had a lot of wisdom he could have shared with me. I wished he could have helped me in understanding girls.

The legacy he left me was a pioneering spirit and a deep love for music. Mom, of course, also helped a great deal. I covet the deep faith he had in God for my children and his love for life and freedom not to be controlled by other's thinking. He was a creative, imaginative person who thought for himself.

Thank you, Dad, for being a tremendous example to me and teaching me to have a freedom in communicating with my children. Thank you God for allowing me to have the mother and father that I had. They were and are the best. I love you.

***

A Reflection of my father

By Anna Wiens Kroeker

The kind of activities that Dad loved to do from day to day that kept him in contact with his family included wandering into the house from room to room to see what everyone was doing. He'd also play soccer and softball with us as he had time. Dad read the Bible to us each day and talked to us about it.

Although my relationship with him was tender and loving - he didn't always understand me. He encouraged me when it was me against my older siblings.

Dad was involved in many community activities. These included acting as a trustee in the Artichoke school board. He was instrumental in bringing power as well as the telephone to the Glenbush area. (Ironically, he never owned a telephone). His church activities involved singing tenor in the church choir and quartet as well directing the junior choir. He was a spiritual example to us though not faultless.

Dad influenced my life in my choice of a mate when he wrote me a letter when I wanted to bring a friend home. He was of a quiet nature and confident spirit which influenced me greatly causing me to want to please him through my actions.

He was humble enough to apologize to others when he was wrong and covered up or protected me from other people's criticism. He was willing to take the blame when others thought we had done something wrong.

He loved harvest time. Dad loved to walk through the grain when it came close to harvesting time. During this time, he would custom combine for others.

He wasn't fussy and ate what was put in front of him thanking God for it. The legacy he left me was his love for children and teens.

His unexpected death made me aware that God is very near at such times and takes care of us. Words of wisdom that he gave me were:

"Don't think that it becomes easier to resist temptation as you grow older because it becomes harder".

A Snapshot of my Father

By Ed Wiens

Writing about Dad is one of the hardest things I've tried to do. The more I think about it and try to formulate my thoughts about him, the more I realize how little I knew him. The thoughts also bring to mind the anger and frustration that I felt when he was taken from us, so early in his life as well as my own. At that time, I had just spent a year at home after graduating from high school. I felt I was just getting to know him as a person – as a friend, instead of as an authority figure who kept me from doing the things I wanted to do.

So at best, my memories of Dad are only snippets of events which I have never been able to interpret to my own satisfaction. I'll try to write some of these down here and maybe together with the shared memories of the rest of you, I will come to understand Dad more fully.

My earliest and I think my fondest memories are of listening to him sing. I remember especially those times when, after I had gone to bed, I could hear him singing the hymns from the German Gesangbuch (song book), with Mom's vibrant accompaniment. The warmth and clarity of his voice are two features I'm still trying to emulate.

He once told me that if people can't understand the words you are singing, then you might just as well not sing. Dad certainly had a large influence on my decision to make singing my career. If I hadn't enjoyed his solos at church as well as his duets with Peter Pauls, so very much, then I don't think that I would have fallen in love with the act of singing. I came to want to express myself, emotionally and intellectually, through song.

I become more and more aware how complex Dad was. He was a man of quick emotions but emotions perhaps kept too much in check. I recall him as a man of deep love and concern for the people around him, but he also had quite a fierce temper, which I think, he had to fight to control more than a few times.

I've seen him become fairly violent with a few mean and stubborn animals. At least once this temper was used in my defense. Reuben and I were walking across the yard to fetch some water from the well when suddenly a young workhorse named Roy came charging around the corner of the barn right at us. I was about six or seven at this time, and in a panic, I threw myself to the ground while Reuben raced for the shelter of the pump. Well, Roy ran right over me, nicked my right thigh with his hoof and ran off. Dad happened to see this, caught Roy, and gave him a good pummeling. I guess it must have been a terrible sight for Dad, to see a horse running right over one of his children. (I still have a two-inch long scar to remind me of this incident).

He certainly cared for his children. I'll never forget the night that he and Mr. Klassen drove me all the way to the Rabbit Lake Hospital to have my stomach pumped to rid it of all the pits that I'd swallowed along with the plums I'd stolen. It was well after midnight, and over very muddy slippery roads. I never got a spanking for that fiasco. I guess Mom and Dad figured I had suffered enough from the sharp stomach pains.

Dad loved to make us laugh. I recall several times that he would tickle Rose until she was quite helpless with laughter. I remember the pleasure of listening in when some of the cousins or older friends came to visit. There always seemed to be a lot of stories told and if I remember correctly, some pretty good storytellers about.

I'm glad the adults tolerated us kids being present during those times. Even though I might not have contributed more than a syllable or two, I still felt very much a part of the company. There was always a lot of laughter in those gatherings.

I believe Dad loved sports, and wanted us to have fun in sporting activities. He encouraged us to play ball, soccer and to ski. However, I have never forgotten the time that he made Reuben and I miss the baseball tournament in North Battleford. Glenbush High School had just won the area championship and we were scheduled to play in the next tournament in North Battleford.

Both Reuben and I were regulars on the team but Dad kept us home to pick roots off some new breaking so he could get it sown before it got too late in the season. I realize the importance of getting the crops in quickly in an area of early frost but I could not understand that this should take precedence over a great event in a boy's life. Maybe that's why I've grown into such an avid baseball fan – I'm getting back at earlier shackles on my enthusiasm.

Another of my memories of Dad involves his sense of community. He was always ready to help someone in need. More than once I watched him leave his combine standing on a sunny day to go spend the afternoon helping a neighbor fix his equipment. I'm sure we can all recall him traveling from neighbor to neighbor in inclement weather in his effort to get the community to sign up for telephone or power services. If Dad ever decided to run for political office, I've no doubt that he would have been easily elected in our community.

One thing I always admired about Dad was his common sense approach to problem solving. He was good with his hands, fixing tired old machinery or building a new wagon or barn. It's too bad he never had the finances to build his dream farm. He certainly worked hard to make a go of it with what was at hand.

I know I will always miss him.

***

In Memory

By Vi Wiens Parris

Dad's death was a sad and tragic event in our lives, but he left us with a heritage never to be forgotten, and many rich memories that will always be a part of my life.

He loved children and demonstrated his affection to us. When we were small, we would often sit on his knees after meals and enjoy a cuddle or a play fight. He was especially affectionate to Blondina as a baby and toddler, cuddling her and walking with her in his arms for many hours as though he was sad that she would be his youngest and last child. He referred to us as 'gifts' from God and thought of himself as blessed quoting Psalms 127: "Sons are a heritage from the Lord, children a reward from him...Blessed is the man whose quiver is full of them."

He enjoyed having fun and would play outdoors with us when he had spare time or on the occasional Sunday afternoon. But he would never play card games or board games – cards (except Rook cards) were representative of the devil, and board games such as monopoly served little purpose or took too long to complete.

Dad had a sense of humor, and he loved to tease, especially his nieces and nephews. When I was in elementary school, he let us all skip school one day to go into town to see a film on sheep ranching in Australia. There must have been eight of us in the blue 1949 Ford eagerly and contently waiting while Dad was in the store and post office looking after some errands.

At the same time, he tried to find out where the film was showing, only to be told that it wasn't on that day. Since it happened to be April 1st, he just came to the car and said this was a big April fool's joke on all of us. We had a good laugh thinking at least we had a day off school, and all this with our parent's permission. To top it off, he then bought each of us a soft drink. What a day!

Whenever possible, he would support us in our activities. Almost every year, he would find the time to attend our track and field sports day, baseball games, Christmas concerts, and special presentations at school. Whenever parents were invited to school events, he would make every effort to be there – even when we were in high school.

He enjoyed suspense and surprise. Christmas was especially an exciting time. Dad would get caught up in the excitement as much as anyone. Traditionally, we would set out our dinner plates on the dining table on Christmas Eve. We believed in Santa, but Dad was the only real Santa.

He made sure there was something fun in our Christmas plates – something we wished for – on Christmas morning rather than only something that was necessary. Gifts were recognized as special, thus we always got more than just "mittens' in our plates. At the end of November, both Mom and Dad would lock themselves in the "blue room" to place a major Christmas order and from then until Christmas morning there was an air of excitement and suspense.

He believed in us, and he expected us to work hard and do our best. We were rewarded for good grades with money – 5 cents for 100%, 4 cents for marks in the 90's, 3 cents for marks in the 80's, 2 cents for marks in the 70's and 1 cent for marks in the 60's. But we had to pay him 1 cent if our marks were in the 50's. If we failed a test, we had to have a good reason, be prepared to do some serious homework, and/or get the strap! Nevertheless, he expressed pride in our accomplishments whether at school or at church. Praise from him was greatly valued and always sincere!

Unlike some parents in the area, after a certain age, he gave us independence in making decisions. At one time, he questioned the content of some harlequin type "nurse" novels that somehow found their way into our house. Since he felt that these books might have questionable content, he felt he should read them. He became rather absorbed in one of the books, sitting in his chair all day reading it from beginning to end. In the end, he decided the content was rather innocuous and did not fall under "banned reading material". Rather, he felt we could make up our own minds on what was good reading and what was not good reading.

The only reading I remember being banned was the so-called "Christian novel", in which a Christian girl meets a non-Christian boy or vice versa; they fall in love, have a stormy romance but always before the end of the book, the non-Christian becomes a Christian and they get married and live happily ever after.

Dad felt this type of story was too unrealistic and went against some of his cherished Christian values regarding dating non-believers. He felt very strongly that believers should not date non-believers. Religious denomination, however, was seldom if ever mentioned as important. Thus these books were banned from my reading until age fourteen, at which time he felt should be mature enough to differentiate between fictional accounts of life and reality itself.

Another time when I was in high school, we had the opportunity to attend a dramatization of *Macbeth*. Since Dad thought it was a movie version and because movies were generally not an acceptable form of entertainment, he was reluctant to give us permission to attend. At that time, he said we were old enough to decide for ourselves whether it was right or wrong for us to attend. I have always respected him for giving us that independence in making choices.

Although he did not always agree with what we did, nor did he always expect us to follow his standards, - he always stood by his own principles. He strongly disagreed with drinking a toast to anyone, as this to him was synonymous with "worldliness" and honoring people rather than God. As a toast to the grads was a part of the banquet, much to my disappointment, he did not attend the banquet, but he was pleased to attend the formal graduation ceremonies immediately after the banquet. Nonetheless, in this instance, he again allowed us the freedom to choose what we thought was acceptable behavior and what was not. We had to decide for ourselves whether to go to the banquet or not.

Music was very important to Dad and many times a source of enjoyment and entertainment. I remember evenings singing with him as he taught me to play the

Autoharp. He would take hymns from the hymnbook and identify chords with numbers so that we could learn to play and sing with the Autoharp.

He also enjoyed gathering people around the piano to sing for hours, just for fun or for practices. He even organized a small orchestra at church for anyone who enjoyed "jamming" with guitars, fiddles, mandolins, piano, Autoharp and voice. Playing and singing as part of this orchestra was a great source of entertainment on a Wednesday or Friday night practice in the wintertime.

I also remember taking this "show on the road" to some nearby village churches. Family singing was especially important to him. Thus he encouraged us to sing melodies as well as parts by learning to read notes. As a result of his efforts, we were invited to sing in some our local church and neighboring churches. I especially remember going to sing in the Battleford Mental Hospital at the age of twelve before a large audience of resident patients.

He encouraged us to learn to read music by notes. He felt this was a more important skill than simply going to the piano and making up tunes or playing familiar tunes by ear.

Music in our house was usually of high quality. We were allowed to listen mostly to classical music, opera and choral music. My father abhorred the twangs and slurs of country and western music. He would change radio stations whenever they started playing this type of music. It didn't matter whether if it was religious or secular programming.

Rock 'n Roll was also generally banned. In fact, he would tell us any music that made one move below the hips was poor quality. Thus it was quite surprising when he came home from town one afternoon and asked if we had ever heard of this Elvis Presley that everyone seemed to raving about. He turned the radio on and searched stations until he heard this supposedly revolutionary musician on the air. He later remarked that Elvis had, in fact, a surprisingly good voice. However, we still grew up listening mostly to opera, oratorio and choral music – mostly the classics.

Because he was a doer rather than a talker, he never suggested someone else should do something that he wasn't willing to do himself, except for preaching at church. This he freely admitted wasn't his gift. But he was quite willing to participate in teaching Sunday school classes and leading the children's choir. However, he never felt that he was irreplaceable. In fact, he suggested that once you felt no one else could fulfill your duties, it was definitely time to resign from the position. Good advice!

His actions were largely responsible for getting electricity to our rural area. Instead of waiting for others to act or simply sitting around wishing we had modern conveniences such as electricity or running water, he put on his cross country skis and skied the area around Glenbush and Rabbit Lake in the cold of winter to get people signed up to commit themselves for paying for the power line to be brought to our area. He was gone for days, coming home only on weekends. People in the area were very neighborly in offering food and shelter to him. Later in 1955, they were certainly appreciative of his efforts when finally the lights went on and we became "modern".

He was always resourceful. No task seemed impossible. He enjoyed learning and was very good in understanding machines and electricity. He would repair farm implements, his own as well as his neighbors. People would come to our place from miles away to see if he could work on some new or old farm implement. He always had time for these people. During the spring and harvest seasons as community members would come to him to get him to repair their equipment, he would get them to drive his tractor or combine while he went to repair their machinery.

He also learned new things quickly. Dad enjoyed working with electricity and helped the electricians wire our house. Learning from them, he then wired other buildings on the farm and in the area. At one time he said that if he were not in farming, he would have been interested in becoming an electrician. He also installed plumbing in our house. Our farm was one of the first to have running water. Dad installed a hot water tank connecting it to the wood stove so that we had hot water whenever the wood stove was lit. Later he also installed similar systems in some of his friends' homes.

For several summers before we had modern refrigeration he took on the role of community butcher for the beef ring so we could have fresh meat in the warm seasons. With the help of Mom, he slaughtered, cut and wrapped local beef once a week in the summer season to be delivered to the participants of the beef ring. Every winter with the help of several couples, he would butcher at least three sows for our family's consumption. This included, naturally, smoking smoked sausages and full hams, rendering lard in a large cauldron outdoors and making it liverwurst. He made the best headcheese and pickled pigs' feet, ears and snout! Little was wasted.

One winter he purchased a shoemaker's sewing machine at a local auction and from thereon in, he repaired all our shoes. He even tried his hand at tanning an animal pelt. When Sport, our family dog died, he thought a dog rug would be useful and look very good on the cold living room floor. The smell of the cleaning and tanning process was absolutely unbelievable, but rug stayed with us for many years, serving as a play rug, an area rug and as a talking piece and reminder of a good dog. It was the most durable rug we ever had!

He often consulted Mom in making decisions, as she seemed to be the one who kept the accounts in order. However, there were a few times when he made decisions alone and seemingly on the spur of the moment. For instance, he came home one late afternoon driving a brand new blue 1949 Ford! I seem to remember my mother was almost speechless, wondering about the wisdom of this purchase.

Another time, I remember one wintry night he came home fairly late from a farm auction. He was much later than expected and Mom was rather anxious at his late arrival. When he finally arrived with the bobsled loaded with household items, two things especially added excitement to his late arrival – our first living room chesterfield and our first RADIO! He connected the radio to a car battery, and thus we had access to another world.

The chesterfield was rather tattered and Mom wondered why he had bought it. He bought it because it was inexpensive and he had the time and the ability to reupholster it – again something he had never done. He did a great job with the remake. Relatives were so impressed with this renewed chesterfield and the talent he showed that he had to reupholster some for them.

Marriage was very important to him. Marriage was an equal partnership. Decisions were usually discussed and made together with Mom. Although I am sure they had their arguments, they were seldom heated and rarely in front of us as children.

Although he didn't talk about his personal faith a great deal, Bible reading and family prayers were very important to him. Thus we always began breakfast with Bible reading and with the exception of seeding and harvesting time, we also ended the day with Bible reading and prayer. The church was very important to him and we went regularly.

All in all, I remember my father for his love of children, his sensitivity and resourcefulness. I regret that he was never able to enjoy being a grandfather to our children. As I grew older, I sense more and more the wisdom and patience he showed in raising us.

***

DAD

By Beth Wiens Friesen

The most outstanding characteristic about Dad in my mind is authenticity. He was what he was, nothing more and nothing less. To me, he represented strength and weakness; silliness and seriousness; affection and abrasion; sensitivity and insensitivity. Really there wasn't very much middle road about him. He was one or the other – definitely not a bland personality.

He would be quite disgusted with us if we made him out to be some perfect saint. I don't think anyone was more aware of his imperfections than he was, yet he espoused confidence, determination and a desire to excel or at least to beat the odds! In my eyes he stood for family, integrity, honesty, commitment and a desire to obey God in all things.

Let me illustrate how I remember these traits being demonstrated in his life.

STRENGTH: When something needed to be done and no one else wanted to shoulder the responsibility, he would do it if he felt it was important. Examples of this: he canvassed communities around us in winter on skis getting people's signatures saying they would support the coming of electricity.

Butchering every week for the beef ring seems like another example too. Also I remember him having to hike to and from Saskatoon (about 150 miles) to get parts for some farm equipment.

Then there was the time a singing group needed to be taken somewhere on an outreach for the church. The day this was to happen, the weather and roads turned bad and no one wanted to drive and so they were going to cancel the whole thing, but Dad said "No Way!" and he drove them.

When it came to bad roads he was never timid in his approach. His philosophy was 'consider your options, make a decision and go for it!' Things might get bumpy but we'll probably make it through somehow! It seems to me that was how he lived his life too.

He seemed very strong to me one day when he found me literally screaming till I was blue in the face and hanging my head between two boards in a boarded up window of Chester's house, unable to help myself. He yelled at Herb to run for a hammer or something, but he didn't wait for it to get there. Instead he tore off a board with his bare hands. It was a pretty impressive performance as far as I was concerned. If I would have known then what I know now I might have called him "Arnold Schwarznagger"!

Another strength he had was the ability to focus and concentrate on something blocking out all other distractions. I remember Mom discussing with us what we should order for him for Christmas while he was in the same room reading a book. He never lifted his head to acknowledge anyone and he hadn't heard a thing about us ordering his presents.

WEAKNESS: At times he would become discouraged and worried about things and be tempted to give up. He was sometimes absentminded and would buy groceries, pay for them, leave them on the store counter and come home without them. He sometimes also seemed to discipline out of impatience rather than patience. This kind of discipline could come in the form of a swift cuff over the ears.

SILLINESS: He loved to tickle us and give us whisker rubs and make us laugh until Mother thought we were going to suffocate to death as so did we!

I remember driving home from visiting someone one Sunday afternoon. Shortly before this, big round ditches were dug along the main road in order to weather proof them. Dad was feeling his 'cheerios' and began to give us all a roller coaster ride by zooming into the ditch on side, back up the road only to go into the ditch on the other side. We were all squealing excitedly while Mother beat Dad on the head with her purse pleading for him to grab hold of his senses. So much for our Disneyland experience!

SERIOUSNESS: He was very often serious about a whole lot of things. When he read the Bible to us and we prayed, we were ALL ALWAYS serious. He had many things to be serious about when it came to running the farm and providing a living.

Sometimes I remember when it was my chore to clear the table after diner. Dad would be sitting at the table deep in thought leaning his head on his hands, just sitting there thinking. I remember this because I always had to walk around him on that side of the table.

One time in particular stands out in my memory because he thoroughly surprised me when he shyly asked me if I was mad at him. I thought he was deep in thought and not even aware of me! And I hadn't realized he was aware of such things when he had so many other important things to try to figure out.

AFFECTIONATE: He loved children and so, of course, children loved him. He loved to hug us and I remember after saying our evening prayers (that was John, Vic, George and me) and the last 'amen' was said we all sprang up like wild little tigers to the be the first one to hug him good night and get our hug and whisker rub.

I remember one other day when we were coming home from school on a very cold late fall day in our horse drawn wagon. We found Dad walking home probably from one of the fields, so we picked him up and because he felt sorry for Vi and me, he opened his big jacket wide and let us snuggle in and get warmed up while he wrapped the coat and his arms around us.

ABRASIVE: To me it seemed that he was never afraid to tell it like it was. I don't remember too many specifics but I remember being told that one time he led a prayer session in church and no one participated, so he finally just said in so many words that if no one had anything to pray about they could pray for him and then he sat down.

INSENSITIVITY: I remember thinking he was insensitive one time when he made some unkind remark to my sisters about how ridiculous he thought my hair looked or other times when he would call my brothers a blockhead if they didn't understand right away what he was asking for when he wanted them to hand him something.

SENSITIVITY: I think I was barely five years old when I had a scary nightmare. I was too afraid to get back to sleep, so I quietly went downstairs to my parents bedside and told Dad that a 'krieg' was going to get me. (I thought a 'krieg' was a monster. Louise Krahn had told us a story in Sunday school about some 'krieg'). Dad turned over and took my little hands into his big hard strong ones and prayed for me that I wouldn't be afraid of a 'krieg' and that I could go back to sleep. I went back to bed and fell asleep immediately.

I think, though, that I must have made too many other trips like this, looking for that special touch from my big daddy, that he got tired of being bothered at night. After coming and telling one night, that I couldn't breathe through my nose or mouth because of a bad cold, he was kind to me but in the morning, I overheard him tell someone that next time he would ram a stick down my throat to open it up so that I would be able to breathe. I don't think I ventured down to his bedside at night ever again. I kind of got the hint!

I think of Dad as something of a romantic for the simple reason that he went ahead and bought something like 300 sheep so that he could learn something about what it felt like to be a shepherd, since there were so many references in the Bible to Jesus being our shepherd.

Another thing I remember about Dad is that he was fairly social, more on a one to one basis than in a group. He loved to visit with friends and neighbors, whether they were Christian or non-Christian.

He was an inventor and seemed very resourceful in solving mechanical problems around the farm. It was like he was never completely stumped for he could always think of something!

One other thing that stood out about him was his eyes. They were deep set with big bushy eyebrows and very expressive. They were either twinkling merrily or flashing snapping and crackling with anger. They would have a cold steely blue look that pierced right through you like daggers. I could never stand up to that look, it alienated me every time but I never got tired of his eyes when they smiled at you and told you that you were okay.

Dad wasn't exactly one of the 10 best-dressed men of the year, but he was not sloppy about his appearances either. I have found memories of watching him apply shaving lotion to his whiskers with his little shaving lotion brush. Of course, I never knew when all of a sudden his hand would leave its usual pathway to his face and suddenly be smothering my face with the lotion instead.

I remember him always wearing either a black or a grey suit and white shirt and tie to church with black polished shoes and a grey hat with a black ribbon around it to church. I thought he was as handsome as any other Glenbush farmer.

At home he almost wore baggy dark navy jeans with a matching jean jacket, car coat length with a heavy black (I think) sweater under it in the winter.

It's funny but I don't remember what a single one of his shirts looked like. But I thought my Dad was the most handsome one Sunday afternoon just shortly after he surprised us all by coming home with about 11 pairs of skates – at least there were a bunch of them. Anyway, it was a Sunday afternoon, early winter or late fall. The slough had frozen over perfectly made for skating and we all headed out to try out our skates, except for Mom and the little girls. The first one out and already with his skates on was Dad. I remember looking up and seeing him gliding effortlessly back and forth in smooth long strides, not only going forwards but backwards too! I have never seen him so beautiful and youthful in my life and I was never as enchanted with him as I was at that moment.

***

REMEMBERING MY DAD, PETER PETER WIENS

By John Wiens

I remember sitting on his knees and he would play Hup-hup-parata with us and just like my children, Michaela and Peter, my younger brothers and sisters would fight to have more than their share of turns.

Often on Sunday afternoons, Dad and us youngest six would walk around and he would sing with us.

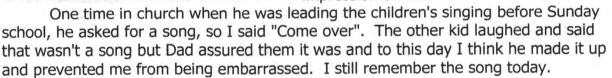

On Sunday afternoons in the winter, he would be out there with us playing soccer.

In winter, I remember John Isaac and Dad sitting and talking together in the Russian language and I thought how funny it sounded. They would also sit and discuss the Holy Scriptures, which has left a positive impression on me.

One time in church when he was leading the children's singing before Sunday school, he asked for a song, so I said "Come over". The other kid laughed and said that wasn't a song but Dad assured them it was and to this day I think he made it up and prevented me from being embarrassed. I still remember the song today.

I think he was a bit of a perfectionist because he couldn't stand grades in school that weren't at least B's. I would receive a royal bum wrap if my report card didn't have any A's or B's.

Dad was definitely a Jack-of-all-Trades. He could tune an engine better than the town mechanic just by listening to a motor. He did the plumbing in our house, the electric wiring, delivering of animals even though he only had a grade ten education.

He was very good at telling stories. He would gather us together for devotions and teach us song after song as well as the Biblical principles – not just the stories. He was very interested in our Christian upbringing.

I think that probably is enough from John the fourth son of Peter Wiens.

Note: John has utilized his love of other languages by traveling to Russia with a mission to work in places such as orphanages and also visited with all the relatives that reside in Russia.

***

A TEN YEAR OLD REMEMBERS

By Naomi Wiens Kapplehoff

I was only ten years old when I lost Dad and these are my memories of him. He and Mom were always in agreement with each other on what we could or could not do. He seemed to know just how we operated. If we wanted to go do some special activity or go somewhere, we'd first go to Mom. If her answer was 'no', we'd go to Dad to see if he would agree with our request. Instead he'd always say 'what did your mother say?' and that was that. He never once to my knowledge went contrary to her decision.

He was compassionate and even merciful. One time I ran (accidentally mind you) into my sister who happened to have a bowl full of very hot water straight off the stove for the purpose of washing dishes. She dumped the water on me which burned my right shoulder. He was the one who took care of the burn.

One year when I was between 7 and 9 I got the mumps just before Christmas. Dad must have suspected it because he had me stay home from school and would you believe it, they were there the next day.

I can still see him in church. One Sunday night on what I guess would be a Christian Endeavor night; he was leading the prayer time and asked if anyone had anything they wanted prayed for. There seemed to be a long silence and I will never forget what he said. "If you have no one to pray for, pray for me".

I loved my Dad as much as any little kid could but I certainly didn't like his discipline. There was a system in church that we all became acquainted with at one time or another to correct behavior problems. In those days, the children sat in the front pews with the women on one side and the men on the other. If we misbehaved (which I did from time to time) we had to sit with mother for a certain period of time.

If that did nothing to mend our little moral consciences, it was Dad we had to sit with and believe me, anything could happen there. There were only one or two times that I can remember that that ever happened. I must have gone to extremes one Sunday sitting next to him because the next thing I remember was being taken out for a spanking and than had to sit in the car for the rest of the services to think about it. What he didn't know was that we would instead spend our time wandering around in the cemetery behind the church. That place fascinated us as kids.

He had a real love for God. This was evident each morning. After breakfast while we were still around the table, he would bring out his Sunday school quarterly and read the morning portion in the German language even though we never understood what he was reading.

His standards especially when it came to school were high. I recall receiving discipline from him because I came home with an "F" on my report card each time in penmanship. Eventually by the time I hit the 8th grade, the teacher raised it to a D.

Now that I am older, I can see that he taught us to take the consequences for our own mistakes. A little red wagon comes to mind when I think about this. It was my job along with Melita and Blondina to bring in enough wood from the woodpile to fill the wood box standing beside the wood stove. The woodpile was in another part of the yard and to get there, you had to climb over a barbwire fence or go through a gate. This wagon was especially useful in getting to the house faster – at least it was faster than carrying it in by the armful. One day we left the wagon in front of the garage. Dad came home with a truck he had borrowed and backed the truck into the garage but in the process he backed right over the wagon. From that time on until we got an electric stove, all the wood had to be carried in by hand. Nice way to learn responsibility!

I don't suppose I will ever forget the day he died. After we younger ones had gone to bed, I heard Ed come in by himself. Mom asked him when Dad was coming and he was the one to tell her that he wouldn't be coming home again because he had been killed in an accident. I wondered what would become of us kids. After I had fallen asleep, Dad came into my dream and told me that everything would be okay.

Perhaps what I missed the most about Dad was school activities such as the annual sports day. He always made it a point to be there. We were given a certain amount of money that we could spend on things such as cracker jacks, ice cream etc. Just before one sports day, I heard girl after girl my age say 'my dad's going to be there' over and over again. That hurt me more than anything else even if I wasn't very athletic because all of a sudden it struck me for perhaps the first time that I was the only girl in the group without a father. It would have been nice to have a father guide me through the rough teenage years.

When I got married, it was sad that he wasn't there to walk me up the aisle. It would have been nice to have my father give me away at my wedding. We missed out on so many things when he died. That day altered our lives forever in more ways that we can account for.

If I could have just one conversation with him, I'd want to know why he had to leave us so soon and I 'd want him to be proud of who I've become today and introduce him to my children and say "THIS IS YOUR GRANDPA!" I would finally freely be able to tell him "I love you Dad!" Just as he told me in my dream so many years ago, things really did turn out okay.

***

August 14, 1992

To My Wiens Cousins:

When I think of your father, my dear Uncle Peter, I think of many years when we had good times together. He took time out to have fun with us younger ones and I recall his cheerful laugh.

Later when I took grades nine and ten in your school district, I lived with your family so I learned to know him better. He usually got up early before 6:00 a.m. He would bring a cup of tea* to Aunt Mary's bedside and go out to do some chores. All summer long he worked hard out on the field.

Sundays were special days when he'd take his family to church where he'd have two or three little ones on his knees and another one or two on either side, all well behaved. On Sunday afternoons, he would gather the family around the piano played by Aunt Mary and everyone would enjoy a great singsong of gospel songs.

I remember Uncle Peter took his place in the church choir in the tenor section. He would often sing solos not only in our local church choir but also at song festivals with other churches together. I remember how I appreciated a series of voice lessons he taught to the young people in our church and in this way encouraged us all to do our best.

I will always think of your father as a favorite person in my life.

Your Cousin,

Marie Enns Penner

- *The cups of tea referred to in this letter were brought to Maria because they helped her get out of bed each morning during per pregnancies. This method really worked.*

Conclusion

I hope that you have enjoyed reading about the life of Maria Derksen Wiens Martens and the people who were important in her life. Through these pages I have tried to capture the essence of who she was and what she meant to many people.

I was watching an interview that Marjorie Gorman Wiens had taped with Mom on the occasion of her 75th birthday. She talked about her upbringing, courtship and marriage. Throughout the conversation between Marjorie and Mom, she always had her hands on her most valuable asset – her Bible. Her Bible meant everything to her. Throughout her life, she had gone through many different ones. One of my sisters described Mom's Bible as being well worn. Her last one was so worn that it was held together with tape.

At the close of the taping, Mom wished to say something that was near and dear to her heart that she desired her children, grandchildren and great grandchildren to know.

Recalling all the difficulties that she had to go through, there was one promise that she stood by. It was her anchor – her mighty oak. She had the assurance found in Hebrews 13: 5. ". . . and be content with what you have, because God has said, "Never will I leave you; never will I forsake you." She moved a few pages forward to James 1:2-7 when she read that all the trials that we go through are meant to develop our character so that in the end we would be mature lacking in nothing. But that through these trials she had the assurance that whatever trial came her way, she had a Savior who would never ever her. He was always walking with her. That promise was her rock. She could said with complete confidence "The Lord is My Helper; I will not be afraid. What can man do to me?" He had never let her down in her long life.

She said that the same God who had held her up for 75 years was a God she could trust and so can we. Her faith in the steadfastness of this God is the legacy she leaves her family.

In conclusion, let me close with a well-known hymn that was written in the 1700's by an unknown person.

How Firm A foundation

1. How firm a foundation, ye saints of the Lord,
    Is laid for your faith in His excellent word!
    What more can He say, than to you He hath said –
    To you, who for refuge to Jesus have fled?

2. "Fear Not, I am with thee, O be not dismayed,
    For I am they God, I will still give thee aid;
    I'll strengthen thee, help thee, and cause thee to stand,
    Upheld by my gracious, omnipotent hand.

3. "When thro' fiery trials they pathway shall lie,
    My grace, all sufficient, shall be thy supply;
    The flame shall not hurt thee, I only design
    Thy dross to consume and thy gold to refine.

4. "The soul that on Jesus hath leaned for repose,
    I will not, I will not desert to his foes;
    That soul, tho' all hell should endeavor to shake,
    I'll never – no, never – no, never forsake"

***

A Strong Woman

A strong woman works out every day
to keep her body in shape.
But a woman of strength kneels in prayer
to keep her soul in shape.

A strong woman isn't afraid of anything.
But a woman of strength
shows courage in the midst of her fear.

A strong woman won't let anyone get the best of her.
But a woman of strength
gives the best of her to everyone.

A strong woman walks sure footedly.
But a woman of strength
knows God will catch her when she falls.

A strong woman wears the look
of confidence on her face.
But a woman of strength wears grace.

A strong woman has faith that
she is strong enough for the journey.
But a woman of strength has faith that
it is in the journey that she will become strong

The author of this poem is unknown

Part Three

Appendix

The Obituary of Peter Peter Wiens

Our beloved husband and father, Peter P. Wiens, was born on January 17, 1908 on a farm near Ufa in Russia. At approximately the age of one year he lost his father. A year later his mother entered a second marriage with Peter H. Pauls.

In May, 1925, at the age of 17, he left Russia with his two sisters, Sara (Mrs. Nicolai Pauls) and Margaret, single at the time. They arrived in Rosthern, where he attended high school for one year. In the summer months, he earned his living by working in Winnipeg and Southern Saskatchewan.

In November, 1927, as a youth, he came to Rev. N. H. Pauls, his brother-in-law's farm at Glenbush, Saskatchewan. Clearing bush land for others was his means of earning wages. At that time he bought a quarter of land.

On September 23, 1928, he was baptized upon the confession of his faith and was received into the fellowship of the Mennonite Brethren Church at Glenbush. During his stay at this place, he was active in the church and the community. In church he enjoyed the Sunday school work and church music activities.

October 7, 1934, he was united in holy matrimony to me, Maria Derksen, at Borden, Saskatchewan. The Lord blessed our marriage and entrusted us with 14 children – 8 daughters and 6 sons. On September 25, 1961 it pleased the Lord to take our beloved husband and father to be with Him in glory. He died as a result of a premature dynamite explosion while he, together with several other men, was removing the foundation of a large water tower, which he and John Isaac had purchased from a railroad company.

He lived to be 53 years, 8 months and 8 days old. I had the privilege of living with him in wedlock for 26 years, 11 months and 18 days. He left to meet sometime in glory his loving wife, Maria; 6 sons, 8 daughters, his 90-year-old mother-in-law; 3 sisters – Sara (Mrs. N. H. Pauls) Kelowna,
B. C., Justina (Mrs. K. K. Siemens) Saskatoon, Saskatchewan, and Margaret (Mrs. J. P. Enns) Vineland, Ontario; 2 half sisters, Tina (Mrs. Peter Warkentin) and Nettie (Mrs. Bernhard Schmidt) both living in Russia and many relatives and friends. Predeceased are his parents, 1 sister, 2 half sisters and one half brother.

In our deep sorrow we find consolation in the words "I will lift up mine eyes until the hills from whence cometh my help. My help cometh the Lord." Ps. 121:1. We are grateful to all who have expressed their sympathy and shown their love in deeds of kindness.

The Bereaved Family

A Final Good-bye to a beloved husband, father & provider

Back row: Herb, Lily, Ed, Vi, Reuben
3rd row: Anna, Mom, Rose, Vic, Beth, John
2nd Row: Naomi, Melita and George
Front Row: Blondina

The final resting place of Peter Peter Wiens in the
Glenbush M.B. Church cemetery

"In Silence We Remember"

- A life lived well
- A Godly example to all who knew him
- Faithful to the end
- A friend to everyone

THE FAMILY OF PETER AND MARIA DERKSEN WIENS

Lily Florence Wiens

Herbert Peter Wiens

Rose Hildegard Wiens

Anna Grace Wiens

Reuben Peter Wiens

Edward Peter Wiens

Violet Viola Wiens

Elizabeth Helen Wiens

John Peter Wiens

Victor Peter Wiens

Gerhard (George) Peter Wiens

Naomi Ruth Wiens

Melita Margaret Wiens

Blondina Johanna Wiens

These are the children
whose lives were impacted and
influenced by the faith and
example of Peter and Maria Wiens.

FATHERS ARE WONDERFUL PEOPLE
By Helen Steiner Rice

Fathers are wonderful people
Too little understood,
And we do not sing their praises
As often as we should . . .
For, somehow, Father seems to be
The man who pays the bills,
While Mother binds up little hurts
And nurses all our ills . . .
And Father struggles daily
To live up to "HIS IMAGE"
As protector and provider
And "hero of the scrimmage" . . .
And perhaps that is the reason
We sometimes get the notion
That fathers are not subject
To the thing we call emotion,
But if you look inside Dad's heart,
Where no one else can see,
You'll find he's sentimental
And as "soft" as he can be . . .
But he's so busy every day
In the grueling race of life,
He leaves the sentimental stuff
To his partner and his wife . . .
But Fathers are just WONDERFUL
In a million different ways,
And they merit loving compliments
And accolades of praise,
For the only reason Dad aspires
To fortune and success
Is to make the family proud of him
And to bring them happiness . . .
And like OUR HEAVENLY FATHER,
He's our guardian and a guide,
Someone that we can count on
To be ALWAYS ON OUR SIDE.

Gerhard (George) Peter Wiens

Gerhard (George) Peter Wiens was born at home on Feb. 13, 1949, the day before Valentines Day. He was the 6th and last son born to Peter and Maria (Derksen) Wiens. He and his two older brothers, John and Vic were often referred to as the 'three little boys'.

As a young boy, he was happy, healthy and inquisitive which sometimes got him into trouble. He loved to ask questions. To encourage the concept of giving to the Lord, each of us children were given some money to drop into the offering plate.

Back in those days, children did not sit with their parents but sat in the very front of the church where they could be seen and not heard. One particular Sunday, the plate came around but he couldn't find his penny. He got up, took his suit jacket off and shook it until the penny fell out.

Another time he decided to experiment with Mother Nature. Our mother and an older brother were at an auction leaving just us young ones at home. As a high wind approached our farm, George with the aid of mother's bread mixing bowl wanted to see how far off the ground he would be lifted. Fortunately for all of us, he came to his senses and was safely in the house before the tornado swept across the yard doing other damage on the yard.

Although George got most of his education in Glenbush, he received one year in Saskatoon. Studying was not a strong suit for him unless you count recess as a subject at which he excelled. He loved sports more than studying. He was an avid hockey player.

He became a Christian as a young child and was baptized in his late teens. He met Edith Neumann in December of 1969. They were married in Chilliwack, B. C. on October 10, 1970. He was hard working and never had any problem finding work. His jobs included Safeway as well as an orchard job which eventually led him to become a concrete pump operator.

During the 8 years that he and Edith were married, George & Edith became the parents of two boys – Ryan (1972) and Joel (1975). He proved to be a good dad who rocked, fed and played with his children. He was a gentle dad who loved to laugh. They lived in various cities eventually settling in Vernon, B. C. where he built a log house for his family.

Sadly, George's life ended on July 4, 1979, when his concrete pump accidentally touched a live electrical wire in Kamloops, B.C. instantly killing him. His boys were six and three at the time. George is buried in Vernon, B. C.

Note: On June 21, 2003, George's son Ryan became a father to a baby daughter named Mary (Tess) Teresa Cameron. Tess's mother is Michelle Cameron.

Viola (Vi) Patsy Willms Wiens
March 16, 1939 – May 1, 1990

Viola ("Vi") Patsy Willms was born to Cornelius and Margaret Willms on March 16, 1939 in Niagara-on-the-lake, Ontario. She grew up in southern Ontario as the oldest of 4 children. She attended Eden Christian High School and was a good student, but she had to leave school early in order to take a job to help her family financially.

When Vi attended Bethany Bible Institute in Hepburn, Saskatchewan, she met Herbert Peter Wiens – also a student there. They were married in Vineland, Ontario on July 7, 1962. They had two children – Howard born on Dec. 28, 1965 and an adopted daughter, Geraldine Jennifer born June 7, 1968.

Vi became a Christian early in life and remained very committed to Christ throughout her adult years. She had a great deal of musical talent which she used in all of the churches she attended. She frequently played piano for the church choir and sang in ladies trios, etc. Her primary hobbies included reading, baking, and supporting her children by attending all of their various sports/music involvements.

During her marriage to Herb, Vi preferred the "background" and enjoyed playing a supporting role in family, social and church functions. However, in 1984 Herb and Vi were separated and subsequently divorced. It was following this event that a new facet of her personality emerged. She became more outgoing and she got very involved in her church's single adult ministry. She became adept at witnessing to her unsaved friends and co-workers. Vi led a number of women to Christ during these years and she excelled at instructing and mentoring these women.

Shortly after her 51st birthday, Vi suffered a sudden seizure which led her to be taken to the Royal Columbian Hospital's Emergency ward in New Westminster B.C. Following some tests, she was diagnosed with a malignant tumor on her brain. She never left the hospital and died 6 weeks later on May 1, 1990. She is buried in Burnaby, B.C.

- submitted by Howard Wiens

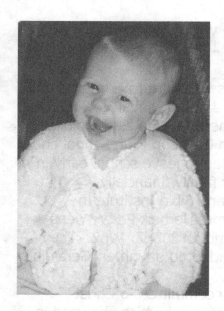

Sadie Lynn Wiggins
April 7, 1999 to October 6, 1999

Daughter of
Dean & Heather (Willems) Wiggins

Granddaughter of
Lawrence & Lily (Wiens) Willems

Great Granddaughter of
Maria Derksen Wiens Martens

July 4, 2003

Dear Sadie Lyn:

I am writing this letter to let you know how you impacted my life. I will never forget when I first felt you move inside me. I remember sitting at work, holding my big belly and feeling happy you were with me. When you were born, I knew you were my "girl", I was so excited to see your face and feel your warm body snuggle against mine. If only I had known that you would not always be with me, that I would never see your first birthday.

I am so glad that I spent everyday of your life with you, holding you and getting to know you. You were so-o special and still are. Your brothers and I feel your presence and live in the comfort that you are with us all the time.

When I took you shopping or to the park, people would stop and admire you. They would comment on what a pretty little girl you are and how your smile was so bright. You caught even the grumpiest person's attention and made them smile. That is what you did best, made people smile.

There is nothing better in this world than to make a positive impact on people you meet and in your short time here you did it to everyone you met and believe me I showed you off to everyone I could find. I was and am so-o proud of you, my pretty angel.

I love to hear your brothers talk about you. Kain holds your pictures and tells you how much he loves you, and Caydon tells me you are "up sun and very happy". I am glad you are in their hearts as you are in mine. We will never forget you and your smile, your laugh, your giggle or your loud squeals.

My dear baby girl, I want you to always know that I miss you and think of you always. You made me happy when you were here and you make me happy now. That will never change. You and I made a bond that can never be broken. Sadie, you are my Angel and shining star, you made a ray of sunlight touch everyone you saw.

Fly Fly little one, Fly beyond imagining
The softest cloud and whitest dove
Upon the wind of heaven's love
Past the planets and stars
Leave this lonely world of ours
Escape the sorrow and pain fly
Remember our promise that
I made to you the day you were born,
We will always love and remember you
With our hearts forever.

I won't forget what you did for me.

With all my Love

Mommy

Maria Georgina Derksen Wiens Martens

Maria Georgina (Wiens) Martens, the daughter of Gerhard and Anna Derksen was born during a blizzard on November 2, 1911 on the farm in Great Deer, Saskatchewan. She was the 11th of 13 children born to this union. At the age of 13 she accepted Christ as her personal Savior and was baptized on August 10, 1928.

Over the years she became a woman of strong faith. She loved to read her Bible and pray and continued this throughout her life. As a child, she taught herself to play the piano and used this talent until the day she entered the hospital. In 1933 she met her future husband, Peter Wiens, while attending a five day music event. They were married October 7, 1934.

They lived in Glenbush, Sask and were blessed with 14 children – 8 daughters and 6 sons. As a pioneer wife, life was difficult for her in the early days, as she was often alone while her husband was working away from home. Sundays were a special day of fellowship with other believers.

July 1, 1959 they celebrated their Silver Anniversary. Two years later, September 25, 1961 Peter was accidentally killed leaving her to raise the seven youngest children. She continued to live on the farm until 1966 when the family moved to Saskatoon. There for the first time she obtained employment at the U of S, working as a housekeeper. She then continued working until retirement, cleaning homes for others.

She married Abram Martens December 30, 1976 and after 23 years of marriage, Abram died on April 18, 1999. In April, 1999 she moved into her apartment at Lutheran Towers where she found life very stimulating and continued using her musical abilities.

Maria died November 17, 2000 at 89 years and 15 days. Her husbands, her parents, 2 brothers, 8 sisters, her son George, one great grandchild Sadie Wiggins and 2 stepchildren, Les Martens and Ruby Martens, predeceased her.

She is survived by daughters, Lily (Lawrence) Willems, Rose (Ernie) Penner, Anna (Ken) Kroeker, Vi (John) Parris, Beth (Ernie) Friesen, Naomi (Phillip) Kapplehoff, Melita (Tim) Kudel and Dina (Russell) Funk; 5 sons – Herb (Lorraine) Wiens, Reuben (Sharon) Wiens, Edward (Donna) Wiens, John (Marjorie) Wiens and Vic (Deanna) Wiens, one daughter-in-law, Edith (Hal) Toews; 2 step-children, Joyce (Wes) Schmidt, Harvey (Marina) Martens, 1 step daughter-in-law Mary Martens; 31 grandchildren, 17 great grandchildren; 1 brother, Henry (Hulda) Derksen, 1 sister, Susie (Jake) Hamm and many nieces and nephews.

Interview with Maria Derksen Wiens Martens

Q. What kind of adjustments did you have to make from living in Borden to moving into a pioneer area?

A. I arrived in Glenbush late at night. It was very dark. It was an all day drive by car from Great Deer to Glenbush. The car your Dad was driving was a borrowed one. The speed limit was about 15 mph and the roads were like one-track roads. We had three flats. At that time you had your own kit and pump along to fix the inner tube and pump up your tire by hand. I don't know how old the car was but we finally made it.

It was a lovely day on October 9, 1934 when I said goodbye to my family. The house that we lived in Glenbush was far from finished on the inside. It was a log house with only stones for a foundation so that the mice could easily come in and I hated that. One time I found a nest in my feather blanket with little mice in it.

Another adjustment was the bedbugs which came out of the wooden boards. Somehow as we plastered and white washed the walls, it was easier to fight the bugs and mice. We bought some kind of powder and powdered all along the walls on the floor and in no time the bugs disappeared. Good thing the bugs did not bite us!

Another was food the first year when we didn't have chickens yet so we didn't have any eggs. But we had milk and fish and some beef.

I came from a house where we were 7 people in one house with a phone and a car. The first winter I was mostly alone in the daytime because Peter was cutting and hauling logs to sell to earn money so that he could buy a plough.

I can't remember missing what I had at home. I loved to read, sew and do fancy work. Then there were some outside chores I had to do. When I came to Glenbush, I was accepted and we had many friends.

Q. How did Dad feel about a large family?
A. He wanted a big family.

Q. How did he feel when one by one his children left the farm to get jobs, education especially when they moved so far away such as Manitoba and B.C.?
A. Because it is normal to leave home when you grow up, it was alright. At that time, everybody who wanted to get a higher education than Grade 12 had to go and work to pay for their education. I remember him asking Rose when she left for B.C. just a few weeks before he was killed, if she would come to his funeral.

Q. What did you do for entertainment in the days before electricity and radio?
A. We did lots of reading, singing, visiting and playing games.

Q. In today's rate of high divorces, what did marriage mean to the two of you, especially when things were really tough?

A. Marriage was a commitment to each other plus a lot of hard work.

Q. What involvement did Dad have in the community and church?

A. He lead the string orchestra, taught Sunday school, sang in the choir and also the male quartet etc.

Q. What was the most important thing that got you through the worst of times such as the loss of the chicken barn on Christmas Eve, droughts and even the loss of a mate or child?

A. Trust in God! God says we are to prove him.

"Test me in this," says the Lord Almighty, "and see if I will not throw open the floodgates of heaven and pour out so much blessing that you will not have room enough for it." Malachi 3:10

A Tribute to Our Mother
Maria Derksen Wiens Martens
November 2, 1911 – November 17, 2000

Mother – what is a mother? The dictionary defines the word "Mother" as a woman who has given birth to a child; a woman exercising control and authority. Maria Derksen Wiens Martens has done that and so much more. In this tribute, we will try to paint a picture of who our mother was and what she meant to us.

> A mother of noble character, who can find
> She is worth far more than rubies or gold.
> Her children arise and call her blessed.

No one's life that we know of, more clearly demonstrated the fruits of the Holy Spirit to us than Mom's did.

LOVE:
Our mom loved us unconditionally. All of us felt it – immediate family, children-in-law, grandchildren and great grandchildren. Not a one of us earned her love. It was just there and we knew it. We were loved unconditionally but never felt smothered by it. And she loved us even when her love was not returned.

She loved our Dad and later on our step-dad. In a day when so many partners work against each other, she did not do this. She and Dad were not always in agreement. Whether she agreed with his opinion or not, she stood by him and him by her. There were times when we would try to get permission for something from Mom. When we didn't get the answer we liked, we would go to Dad thinking he might not be as informed with all the details. But more often than not his answer was "What did your mother say". This, of course, was the end of the discussion. They found ways to settle their differences but it was rarely in from the children.

Mom loved to learn. She had an 8th grade education. When she finished school, she finished with the highest marks in Saskatchewan and received a certificate to prove it. She wanted to go to high school but family finances did not let that happen, as she would have had to board out in another home and another town. But she certainly didn't let the lack of a high school diploma stop her from learning.

She read a lot of books and encouraged her children to get as much education as possible. She encouraged us to go on when we felt like quitting and reminded us that the goal was worthy of the effort. She stressed the value of education rather than just getting another job.

LONG-SUFFERING:
Mother showed us how not only to suffer for a long, long time, but also to endure - how to work through very difficult times with gracefulness, determination, and true grit. This is where she achieved the extraordinary by doing the ordinary and on a

consistent basis. Never making a show of things, just keeping on going, and going and going

Mother faced many challenges in her life. She faced the challenge of going from her parents home of many people, to the loneliness of being the wife of a pioneer raising children, but none was as challenging as the role she was forced to take on at the age of 49 when her whole world turned upside down and inside out.

On the night of September 25, 1961, she knew without being told when she saw Ed walking in from the car by himself, that her beloved husband was never coming home again. The responsibility of completing the rearing of 7 children under the age of 17 now fell on her shoulders.

Her strength and courage became evident in ways that we had never seen before. More than ever, she depended on the Lord to get her through this period. When she could easily have lost her temper and given into her frustrations with us, especially as we entered our teens, she did not – and this is much to be admired.

GENTLENESS:

Consider this! Here was a woman who raised 14 children and every one of us, including all her children-in-law and grandchildren, to a man – think of her as a gentle and a quietly caring woman. This was one of her most endearing characteristics. We will always remember her for her gentleness, in spite of and probably because of her great inner strength.

Music played a big part in her life and consequently got transferred to us. She was a self-taught pianist. Once she was having trouble getting a certain beat. She worked and worked on it but just didn't understand it. When she woke up, she went to the piano and sure enough, she was able to play this particular beat as she had felt it in her dream.

JOY:

Mother wasn't happy all of the time but she had in her an underlying river of joy which carried her throughout her entire life. When she played the piano, her joy poured out of her hands, body, voice and face filling our entire house.

She received each one of us with joy from the day we were born to her last breath. She once said that she never felt that a new baby was just another addition or an added burden.

Sunday afternoons were often spent in the living room with Mother at the piano singing hymns and other songs that we liked. Only those who wanted to join her, but probably 80% of the time 90% of the family, eventually found their way to the piano to join her. At one time there was even a band – Mother on the piano, Dad on the autoharp or guitar and other neighbors on other instruments. It didn't matter if they were out of tune or not – to our ears this was music!

She also served as the pianist of the Borden church choir. For many years early in her married years, she juggled caring for whatever baby she had at the time with playing the piano for the church choir at Glenbush.

In her last years, she was memorizing whole pieces of music so that she would be able to continue to play her piano if and when she began losing her eyesight.

Mother also played the piano for the senior citizen retirement home she lived in. The day she went to the hospital, realizing full well that she would almost surely not return, she had the presence of mind to notify those in charge that she would not be able to keep her commitment to play for them that day.

Mom loved a good laugh and we loved to hear her laugh. So did Dad, who would on occasion tickle her mercilessly! One year, when Vi came home for Christmas, with no ring or guy but just a slide of her intended, her little sister announced that Vi was engaged! Mom's response was "to what - her teaching?"

Our cousin Peter Enns, who boarded with our family during the winter when Lily was in Grade One, had the job of driving Lily to school on the cutter. The horse he had to drive one day was a horse named Frank. Frank was one of the slower horses. Peter and Lily pulled up in front of the gate but Frank didn't want to stop. So Peter took out his long 20-foot whip and just raised it …Frank took off, pulling the runners off, leaving Peter and Lily sitting in the now disabled cutter! Mom was watching from the window and enjoyed a great laugh.

PEACE:

Even though we gave our mother way more than her share of worries, she was able to claim God's peace in her life. When our dad died, her peace was very evident - even in her pain. There were things that agitated her, to be sure, but she found her way through them. And again, nothing filled our home with a peaceful feeling better than when she played the piano. After a day of hard work keeping all of us organized, as well as dealing with the hazards and insecurities of life on the farm in the far north, she filled our home with her peaceful acceptance of whatever came her way.

PATIENCE:

There were things that Mom had no patience for at all! One was when we wanted to give up. Give up on a job not completed. Give up on ourselves and a belief that we could achieve. Or give up on our personal goals. Especially when it came to completing university or other courses we started.

Laziness or boredom was something that was never allowed. If we were bored, you could be sure that she found something to do with our time, and more often than not especially in the summer, she would send us to the garden to do some weeding – a task some of us did not like.

She also believed that allowances were not handed out without reason – we earned them. Some the children got a penny for every fresh gopher that they got, others got nickels for memorizing entire hymns. Her motto for life was "If there's a will, there's a way!" Somehow she found a way to accomplish these goals – each child was different and therefore in her mind, there were 14 different ways to accomplish the desire goal.

Looking back, we can plainly see how amazingly patient she was with each of us, letting us grow at our own pace. Letting us make mistakes, always ready to encourage us to keep going. Forgiving us for our lack of communication as well as our lack of not sharing encouragement with her; always accepting us without recriminations, and finally, patiently but persistently loving us unconditionally.

KINDNESS:

I doubt whether anyone could accuse Mother of an unkind deed. She very kindly took us in, as well as anyone else, whenever we appeared at her door. She was always prepared to serve a meal for however many people there were – even for hungry old Mr. Chester, who could probably smell the great meals Mom made from a mile away as he chugged along in his old truck at 5 mph on his way to Glenbush.

As each of us eventfully married, Mother accepted each and every one of our mates with the same kind of love she gave to us. Mother never gave advise to us during marriage about how to do things or how we should raise our children, even when our methods were different from what she would have done. She again with the help of God, kept her thoughts to herself. She waited until we came to her for advice.

GOODNESS:

Mother was good, through and through. Here are some statements written by us, her family, as a tribute to her on her 80th birthday. Thanks to Naomi, we were able to tell HER how wonderful she really was while she was still with us.

- Your days were long and demanding but you never complained.
- Thank you for teaching and showing us the way to God.
- Thank you for praying for our children and us.
- The food you made was always plentiful and very delicious.
- With all the work you had to get the family ready for church, we should have been the last, but no, most of the time we were one of the first to arrive.
- You have been most influential in our lives in your devotion and trust to God.
- Thank you for standing by us without judgment.
- Even when we failed and rebelled, you showed great love and care.
- You always had a smile for us.
- You expected the best from us.
- Your organization and managing skills were exquisite.
- You were such a hard worker.
- Your heart was always open to hear.
- No one could have had a more adequate mother.
- You accepted tasks and simply did them, knowing how to prioritize. (This included prioritizing her values. She demonstrated this in the early 50's by asking our church to consider holding the evangelistic services they held each year, in English, rather than German for the sake of the English speaking community we were part of. However the powers that be didn't agree with her and German prevailed.)
- Your worries and concerns never seemed to paralyze your efforts.
- Her faith in you, Lord, when times were tough, helped us know we can depend on you.

- 234 -

- You were such a steady and thorough person that the decisions you made were wise ones.
- You leave us with images of your ready smile and loving, helping arms.
- You took such joy in preparing our Christmases and making that wonderful Easter bread – paska.
- Every evening, when we were young, you read us a story and prayed with us.
- Your discipline was always consistent.
- I never understood you as a parent until I became one.
- You have constantly reminded us to look to The Maker, rather than dwell on the problem.
- We admire the way you have stood by us and loved us regardless of our mistakes and blunders.
- Thank you for showing us how to control our tongues.
- We will always remember your softness.
- We value your great insight in reading people's character. You were right about them all!
- We enjoyed the calming effect our visits had on us.
- Thank you for always stressing the importance of education.
- How did you remember everyone's birthday?
- Your gift of hospitality has been a great example.
- No one left your house hungry.
- You welcomed us in at any time, and put up with a lot of noise and mischief.
- Matthew knew the route to your house before he was a year old and would scream if we didn't turn right onto Idyllwyld by the Travelodge.
- Thank you for your loving help and encouragement.

You have waited with patience when it was needful
Yet kept no person waiting for yourself
And of all others' troubles have been most heedful
But have hidden your own sad stories on the shelf
Nothing less than what was best could win you.

We would all, every one of us, be thoroughly complimented if anyone every said to us "You are just like your Mother!"

A Tribute to Mrs. Maria Wiens Martens

Here we are under the dome of an open sky, and momentarily this place becomes sacred and solemn.

I snap to attention and salute, for we are about to lie to rest a patriarchal matron, a prodigy of a valiant pioneering family of this community. She was one of the few remaining offspring of those early stalwart settlers. Her spirit is with us: her earthly life has ebbed away. She lay before us with her snowy white hair that demands our respect.

Her giftedness in the aesthetic things of life was recognized by her parents. Music was an expertise that she developed early in life. As a young lad I can remember her pumping away at the bellows of the church organ. In her home and soon in the church her fingers ran deftly across the keyboard of the piano. She followed the baton that pleased the musical masters. It was at a festival of music that her suitor saw her and in his nervousness, he dropped the baton. For many years she played for the choir and the general singing of the congregation here in the Borden church. To develop this expertise in those early pioneering days was no easy matter.

All of us in the Derksen clan have a heritage that is rooted in rock solid Biblical principles. This has produced a family of thirteen godly God-fearing men and women of faith. At age fourteen Maria internalized and personalized this faith that has manifested itself in overt outward actions for the last seventy-five years.

We all do well to emulate a faith that has endured the hills and valleys that are characteristic of life as we experience it. She has finished well and received a rich welcome into the eternal Kingdom of our Lord and Savior Jesus Christ. To my mind it is unconceivable that any young couple would deliberately plan to have a quiver so full that would produce fourteen children. As a slim, young, beautiful homemaker the reproductive process began. Each child was loved, nurtured and received as a gift from God.

By her own confession she writes that she viewed her family as a trust from God, eight daughters and six sons. I believe that her character can be summarized in two words, namely SHE PERSEVERED. Just think of the magnitude of these two words when at any given time during the first twenty five years of her marriage there was a baby cooing and crying in a crib, the feet of some toddlers pattering on the kitchen floor, two raucous preteens wresting on the living floor and graciously dealing with some moody, mood swinging teens. She persevered indeed and today, as always, her children rise up and call her blessed.

Indeed without flattery she was a woman of noble character. Her husband had full confidence in her. She worked eagerly with her hands to provide for her household. What she did, she did with vigor - her arms and hands were equal to the task. At times her lamp would burn late into the night. She lived beyond herself opening her arms to the poor and extending a hand to the needy. When the cold blasts of winter blew she had no fear, for her children were clothes with parkas.

Her husband took his place among the leaders of the community. She ran an orderly household, a place for everything and everything in its place. I believe her family would concur that she spoke with wisdom, and faithful instruction came from her lips.

Charm is deceptive and beauty is fleeting, but a woman who fears the Lord is to be praised.

A righteous woman shall be remembered forever!

We give her the accolades she deserves. AMEN.

I Cor. 15:50-58

Otto Derksen

PART 4

Appendix

Bibliography

Cover art: "The Gateway to Heaven" by Phillip Kapplehoff ©2003

Martin, I G. "*I Will Meet You in The Morning*". Crowning Glory Hymnal. Singspiration® Inc. Zondervan Publishing House. 1967

Black, James M. "*When the Roll is Called Up Yonder*". Crowning Glory Hymnal. Singspiration® Inc. Zondervan Publishing House. 1967

_____Reciprocity Treaty, 1911. Available: www.mta. ca/faculty/ arts/canadian_studies/english/about/study_guide/debates/ receiprocity. html.

Maps courtesy of www.fact-index.com/h/hi/history_of_canada.html

Derksen, Anna. "Something About the Grandparents Derksen".

 ____The Gerhard G. Derksen Family Book. Friesen Yearbooks, Altona, MB. 1984.

Crosby, Fanny. "*Blessed Assurance*". Crowning Glory Hymnal. Singspiration® Inc. Zondervan Publishing House. 1967

_____Canadian Map courtesy of www.fact-index.com/h/hi/history_of_canada.html.

Borden Mennonite Brethren Church. Precious Memories. 1905 – 1980. Friesen Printers. Altona, Manitoba. Canada

Borden Mennonite Brethren Church. Available: www.mbconf. ca/ mb studies/ holdings/sk/Borden.en.html.

Canadian Treaties Map courtesy of www.collectionscanada.ca/confederation/ Kid/h2-1450-e.htlm

____Canadian Conference of Mennonite Brethren Churches. Available: http://encyclopedia.thefreedictionary.com

_____"The Evolution of Newspapers". Available: www.cna-acj. ca/ client/ cna.nsf/ web/Facts

_____"Winnipeg Free Press – Partners in Progress": Available: www.winnipeg freepress.com

Borden History Book Committee. OurTreasured Heritage – Borden & District ©1980

_____"Battles:The Battle of Vimy Ridge. 1917" Available:
   www.firstworldwar.com/battles/vimridge.htm.

CBC News: Flu Epidemic. Available: www.cbc.ca/news/indepth/background/sars_
Epidemic.htlm.

Ricketts, Bruce. The Spanish Flu. Available: www.mysteriesofcanada.com

_____Spanish Flu. Available: www.fact-index.com/s/sp/spanish_flu.html

_____Influenza in the First World War: Available:
   www.spartacus.schoolnet.co.uk/FWWinfluenzia.htm.

___Spanish Flu 1918: History's Faster Killer Pictures of Spanish Flu: Available:
www.glacombe.com/flu.htlm

Morrison, Van. "*Old Black Joe*". Available: www.lyricsBox.com ©2002-2004

_____"Russian Revolution". Encyclopedia Americana vol.24. Grolier Inc.
Danbury,   Conn. 1989

_____"The Bolsheviks" Available: www.dur.ac.uk

_____"The History Guide. Lectures on Twentieth Century Europe. "The Aftermath of the
   Bolshevik Revolution". Available: www.History guide.org/Europe/lecture7.html.

Peterson, John W. "*It Took a Miracle*". Crowning Glory Hymnal.
Singspiration® Inc. Zondervan Publishing House. 1967

Guenther, Bruce L. "The Historical Roots of Bethany College".
Available: www. Mbconf.ca/historian/02-09/feature-1.en.html.

_____ Bethany Bible Institute – Celebrating God's Faithfulness.
© Copyright 2002 Bethany Bible Institute.

 _____ "Alcohol Prohibition". Available: www.collections.ic. gc.ca/cree/ pioneer/ Booze

_____Intemperance. Available: www.hoboes.com/html/ Politics/ Prohibition/
   Notes/Intemperance.html.

_____"Prohibition in the 1920's: Thirteen Years That Damaged America". Available:
   www.geocities.com/athens/Troy/4399

_____"Alcohol (1958)": Available: www.mhsc.ca/encyclopedia/ contents/ A4385ME. html.

Schreckengast, Rachel Sandfordyln. History of Engagement Rings. www.wedfrugal.com

Cairns, Earl E. Christianity Through the Centuries. Grand Rapids, Mich. Zondervan Publishing House.   1954.

Dober, Dusko., National Geographic. "The Bolshevik Revolution". October, 1992

Dyck, Cornelius J. An Introduction to Mennonite History. Herald Press. 1967.

Encyclopedia Americana. Danbury, Conn. Grolier, Inc. Vol. 18 and 24, 1989

_____Mennonite and Taxes. Available: www.mhsc.ca/encyclopedia/contents

_____Mennonite and Nonresistance. Available: www.mhsc.ca/ encyclopedia/ contents

_____Who are the Mennonites: Menno Life: Available: www.thirdway.com /menno/lite

_____Encylopedia Americana Vol. 25. p. 637.

_____The Trails of Promise. Friesen Printers. Altona, Manitoba. 1984.

_____The church records of the Glenbush M.B. Church. Glenbush, Sask.

Pauls, Nicolai P. Notes from 25th Anniversary of Glenbush M.B. Church 1952.

_____Ufa: The Mennonite Settlement. 1977

Letters from Peter Wiens to Maria Derksen dated December 20, 1933, August 7, 1934 and August 18, 1934.

Wistrich, Robert. Jewish Virtual Library. Adolf Hitler. Available: www.jewishvirtual Library.org/jsource/Holocaust/Hitler/html. Copywrite 2004.
The American-Israeli Cooperative Enterprise.

_____Adolf Hitler. Available: www.remember.org/guide/Facts.root.hitler.html. Copywrite 1990. Gary M. Grobman.

European Maps:
_____ Europe in the 1920's. Available: www.nfgl-cymru.org.uk.

_____Interwar Europe. Available: www.users.erols.com/ mwhite28.euro 1935.htm.

_____ "Canada's Role in WWII". Available: www.canadaka.net

_____"The Canadian Women's Army Corp". Available: www.junobeach.org.

_____"The Women's Army Corps: A Commemoration of World War II Service". Available: www.army.mil.

_____World War II: Combatants and Casualties (1937-45). Available: http://web.jjay.Cuny.edu/-jobrien/reference.0b62.html.

_____Japanese Internment Camps. Available: www.yesnet.yk.ca /schools/ projects/canadianhistory/camps/internment1.html.

_____The Crucible: Military Might. Available: http://history.cbc.ca/history

_____The Crucible: The American Cousin. Available: http://history.cbc.ca/history

Wikipedia. "Baby Boomer". Available: www.fact-index.com /b/ba /baby_ boomer

Chui, Tina. "Canada's Population Charting Into the 21st Century". Statistics Canada – Catalogue 11-008-XPE. Canadaian Social Trends –Autumn 1996.

_____ Key Economic Events: "1944 – Family Allowance Program: Supporting Canadian Children". Available: http://canadianeconomy. gc.ca/english/ economy/1944family.html.

_____"That Was Then ...": First 'baby bonus' cheques mailed. Available: http://archives.cbc.ca/400i.asp?IDCat=73&IDDos=206&IDCi=1031&IDLan=1&type=he bdoclip.

_____O Gladsome Light, O Grace. Available: www.geocities.com/Heartland/Hills/ 2168/lyrics/song180.html.

Christian History Institute. Issue #29: Charles Wesley: Heart of the Evangelical Revival. Available: www.gospelcom.net /chi/GLIMPSEF/glimpses /glmps029.shtml.

_____Charles Wesley. Available: www.smithcreekmusic .com/ hymnology/ Wesleys/Charles.Wesley.html.

_____Frances Jane Crosby. Available: www.cyberhymnal. org/bio/c/r /crosby_ fj.htm.

Christian History Institute. Issue #30: Fanny Crosby: Queen of American Hymn : www.gospelcom.net/chi/GLIMPSEF/Glimpses/glmps030.shtml.

Osbeck, Kenneth W., 101 Hymn Stories. Kregel Publications. Grand Rapids, MI. © 1982 by Kenneth W. Osbeck.

Wesley, Charles. "*O for a Thousand Tongues*". Crowning Glory Hymnal. Singspiration® Inc. Zondervan Publishing House. 1967

Crosby, Fanny. "*All the Way My Savior Leads Me*". Crowning Glory Hymnal. Singspiration® Inc. Zondervan Publishing House. 1967

Author Unknown. "*He Is Lord*".

Author Unknown. "*God is Good*.

Author Unknown. "He Maketh No Mistake". Available: www.webedelic.com

Joyner, Jeff. "*I Will Rest in You*". Used by the permission of Jeff Joyner. ©2002 Jeff Joyner, JT Music.

Huntington, D. W. C. "*The Home Over There*". Crowning Glory Hymnal. Singspiration® Inc. Zondervan Publishing House. 1967

Author Unknown. "*How Firm a Foundation*". From Rippon's "Selection of Hymns". Crowning Glory Hymnal. Singspiration® Inc. Zondervan Publishing House. 1967

"Sadie" by Phillip Kapplehoff ©2004

Foot Notes

Chapter 7
1. Guenther, Bruce L. "The Historical Roots of Bethany College".
   www.mbconf.ca/historian/02-09/feature-l

Chapter 8
2. Ufa: The Mennonite Settlement. 1977.

Chapter 9
3. Encylopedia Americana Vol. 25. p. 637.

Chapter 11
4. Card from Rosella Klassen Martens dated Octber 4, 2004.
5. The entire notes of Nicolai Pauls used on the 25th Anniversary of the Glenbush
   M.B. Church.

Chapter 12
6. The Gerhard G. Derksen Family Book. Altona, Manitoba:
Friesen Printers. 1984

Chapter 13
7. ibid

Chapter 15
8. Christian History Institute. Issur #30: Fanny Crosby: Queen of American Hymn
   Writers. www.gospel.com.net/chi/GLIMPSEF/Glimpses'glmps030.shtml

9. Frances Jane Crosby. www.cyberhymnal.org/bio/c/r/crosby_fj.htm

Chapter 17
10. Letter dated August 17, 1976 from Maria Wiens to Dina Wiens.

Printed in the United States
By Bookmasters